Reading STREET

Program Authors

Peter Afflerbach

Camille Blachowicz

Candy Dawson Boyd

Wendy Cheyney

Connie Juel

Edward Kame'enui

Donald Leu

Jeanne Paratore

P. David Pearson

Sam Sebesta

Deborah Simmons

Sharon Vaughn

Susan Watts-Taffe

Karen Kring Wixson

PEARSON

Scott Foresman

Editorial Offices: Glenview, Illinois • Parsippany, New Jersey • New York, New York
Sales Offices: Boston, Massachusetts • Duluth, Georgia • Glenview, Illinois
Coppell, Texas • Sacramento, California • Mesa, Arizona

We dedicate Reading Street to
Peter Jovanovich.

His wisdom, courage,
and passion for education
are an inspiration to us all.

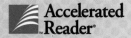

About the Cover Artist

Mark Buehner's sisters say that he was born with a pencil in his hand. While he was growing up, pulling out pencils, paper, and watercolors was part of his daily routine. He loved poring over the pictures in books and even used to staple his pictures together to make books. He had no idea that what he was doing would eventually become his career. He grew up to become an award-winning illustrator of books for children. He believes he has the best job in the world!

ISBN-13: 978-0-328-24351-8
ISBN-10: 0-328-24351-5

4 5 6 7 8 9 10 V057 16 15 14 13 12 11 10 09 08
CC:N1

Dear Reader,

Are you enjoying your trip down *Scott Foresman Reading Street?* We hope you are ready for more reading adventures. This book is about being unique, about cultures, and about freedom. You will read about the world record breakers on planet Earth. You will read about the Statue of Liberty and about two ants who run away. You will meet children who live all over the world.

At each intersection, you will learn something new. But you will also have many chances to use what you learned before. We hope you have fun in the process.

Buckle up and enjoy the trip!

Sincerely,
The Authors

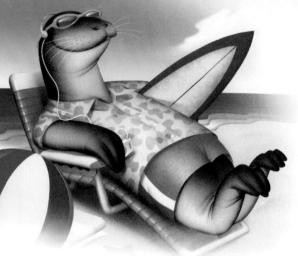

ONE of a Kind

What does it mean to be unique?

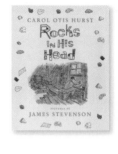

CULTURES

What happens when two ways of life come together?

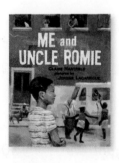

Freedom

What does it mean to be free?

ONE of a Kind

What does it mean to be unique?

Wings

A unique boy overcomes
loneliness.

FANTASY

connect to
SOCIAL
STUDIES

Hottest, Coldest,
Highest, Deepest

There are many unique places
around the world to learn about.

EXPOSITORY NONFICTION

connect to
SCIENCE

Rocks in His Head

A man makes use of
his unusual hobby.

BIOGRAPHY

connect to
SCIENCE

America's Champion
Swimmer:
Gertrude Ederle

Gertrude Ederle becomes the
first to do what she does.

BIOGRAPHY

connect to
SOCIAL
STUDIES

Fly, Eagle, Fly!

A unique eagle thinks
he is a chicken.

FOLK TALE

connect to
SCIENCE

11

Wings

Comprehension

Skill
Cause and Effect

Strategy
Answer Questions

Cause and Effect

- A cause tells *why* something happened.

- An effect is *what* happened.

- *Because* and *so* are clue words that show a cause and an effect. Sometimes a clue word is not used.

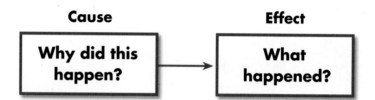

Cause		**Effect**
Why did this happen?	→	**What happened?**

 ## Strategy: Answer Questions

Good readers know where to look to answer a question. Sometimes the answer is right there in the text. At other times you must think and search. You may need to look in different parts of the text. You can do this when you ask yourself the questions, "What happened?" and "Why did it happen?"

Write to Read

1. Read "A Dragon's Tale." Make a graphic organizer like the one above for each cause and effect that you find.

2. Answer this question: "What happened when Drew said 'Hi' to the turtle?" Then tell where you found the answer.

A Dragon's Tale

One morning Drew D. Dragon went searching for someone to play with. High in a tree he spotted a robin. "Hello," he said to the robin. Whoosh! Crackle! The fire in Drew's breath burned the leaves off the tree. The robin squawked and flew away.

Later, in a pond, Drew noticed a turtle. "Hi!" Drew said to the turtle. Whoosh! Crackle! The fire in his breath made the pond boil. The turtle jumped out of the hot water, pulled its head and feet into its shell, and stayed there, looking like a rock.

Drew sighed and leaned against a tree. He was just about to say, "I guess I'll play by myself," when he heard someone say, "I guess I'll play by myself." On the other side of the tree, he saw a dragon, and she was about his age.

"I want to play with someone, but I just scare everybody off because of my breath," DeeDee Dragon explained.

"Hey, I have the same problem!" said Drew. "Would you like to play with me?"

So DeeDee and Drew joked and laughed and rolled down hills. They baked apples by breathing on them and became the best of friends.

Skill Something has happened here. There's no clue word, but can you tell what caused the robin to squawk and fly away?

Strategy How would you find the answer to this question: Why wouldn't anyone play with DeeDee? Look in this paragraph.

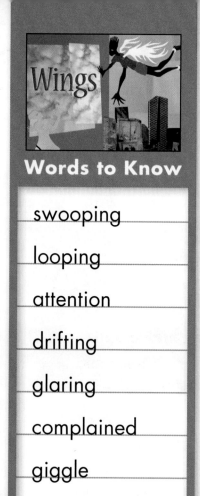

Wings

Words to Know

swooping

looping

attention

drifting

glaring

complained

giggle

struggled

Remember

Try the strategy. Then, if you need more help, use your glossary or a dictionary.

Vocabulary Strategy
for Endings

Word Structure Sometimes when you are reading, you may come across a word you don't know. Look closely at the word. Does it have the ending *-ing*? The ending *-ing* is usually added to a verb, or action word. You may be able to use the ending to help you figure out the meaning of the word.

1. Put your finger over the *-ing* ending.

2. Look at the base word. Do you know what the base word means?

3. Try your meaning in the sentence. Does it make sense?

Read "The Story of Daedalus and Icarus." Look for words that have the ending *-ing*. Use the ending to help you figure out the meanings of the words.

14

The Story of Daedalus and Icarus

The ancient Greeks told a story about Daedalus who was a very clever inventor. When he and his son Icarus were imprisoned on an island, Daedalus invented a way to escape. With feathers, thread, and wax, he made two pairs of wings. Then he and Icarus flew away.

Icarus, excited to be flying, began swooping down toward the sea, looping around his father, and zooming up toward the sun.

"Icarus," Daedalus warned, "don't fly too high or the sun will melt the wax on your wings. And don't fly too low or the sea will dampen the feathers."

But Icarus paid no attention. He kept soaring higher and higher and drifting closer and closer to the hot, glaring sun.

"Icarus!" Daedalus shouted. "Come back right now!"

"I never get to have any fun," Icarus complained. With a giggle, he made another high arc.

Suddenly his wings wobbled. Icarus struggled to stay in flight, but it was too late. The heat from the sun had melted the wax that held his wings together. Icarus fell into the sea and drowned.

Words to Write

Write a description of what you think it would be like to fly like a bird. Use words from the Words to Know list.

Wings

BY CHRISTOPHER MYERS

Genre A **fantasy** is a story in which unbelievable things happen. Why is this story a fantasy?

Are these wings the only thing
that makes this boy special?

"Look at that strange boy!" Everyone from the neighborhood is pointing fingers and watching the sky. "How's he doing that?" They stretch their necks and shake their heads. Ikarus Jackson, a new boy on my block, is flying above the rooftops. He is swooping and diving, looping past people's windows and over the crowd. I don't think he's strange.

Ikarus Jackson, the fly boy, came to my school last Thursday. His long, strong, proud wings followed wherever he went.

The whole school was staring eyes and wagging tongues. They whispered about his wings and his hair and his shoes. Like they whisper about how quiet I am.

Our teacher complained that the other kids couldn't help but gawk and stare. He said that Ikarus's wings blocked the blackboard and made it hard for the students to pay attention.

The teacher told Ikarus to leave class until he could figure out what to do with his wings. He left the room quietly, dragging his feathers behind him. One boy snickered.

At recess the snicker grew into a giggle and spread across the playground. Soon all the kids were laughing at Ikarus Jackson's "useless" wings. I thought that if he flew just once everyone would stop laughing. Ikarus looked up, flapped his wings a couple of times, then jumped into the air.

He swept through the schoolyard like a slow-motion instant replay.

But the other kids were not impressed. One girl grabbed the basketball. A boy stuffed the handball in his pocket. Somebody nagged, "Nobody likes a show-off."

Their words sent Ikarus drifting into the sky, away from the glaring eyes and the pointing fingers. I waited for them to point back at me as I watched Ikarus float farther and farther away.

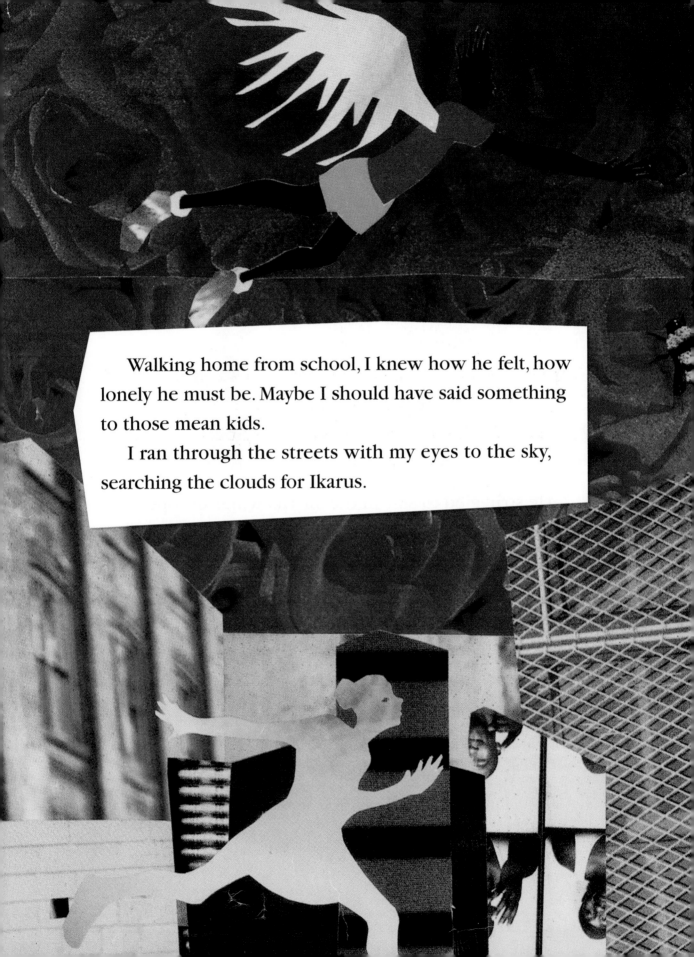

Walking home from school, I knew how he felt, how lonely he must be. Maybe I should have said something to those mean kids.

I ran through the streets with my eyes to the sky, searching the clouds for Ikarus.

He struggled to stay in the air. His wings drooped and his head hung low.

He landed heavily on the edge of a building and sat with the pigeons. Pigeons don't make fun of people.

A policeman passing by blew his whistle. "You with the wings, come down from there! Stay yourself on the ground. You'll get in trouble, you'll get hurt."

It seemed to me Ikarus was already in trouble and hurt. Could the policeman put him in jail for flying, for being too different?

When the neighborhood kids saw the policeman yelling at him, they exploded with laughter. Ikarus dropped to the ground. "Stop!" I cried. "Leave him alone." And they did.

I called to Ikarus and he sailed closer to me. I told him what someone should have long ago: "Your flying is beautiful."

For the first time, I saw Ikarus smile. At that moment I forgot about the kids who had laughed at him and me. I was just glad that Ikarus had found his wings again.

"Look at that amazing boy!" I called to all the people on the street as I pointed to my new friend Ikarus swirling through the sky.

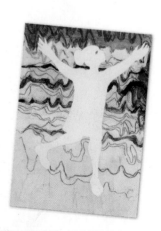

Reader Response

Open for Discussion If Ikarus came to your school, how would you treat him? Tell a story about Ikarus and you.

1. What other stories do you know in which people fly? What reasons might authors have for making up such stories? Think Like an Author

2. When Ikarus Jackson is sad, his wings droop and his feathers drag. What causes Ikarus to feel so sad? Cause and Effect

3. The main character is very brave to say, "Stop! Leave him alone!" Why does she risk being kind to Ikarus? Where did you find the answer? Answer Questions

4. Pretend you are a newspaper reporter walking down the street as Ikarus Jackson flies over. Write an account for your paper. Use words from the Words to Know list and from the story. Vocabulary

Look Back and Write What should someone have said to Ikarus long ago? Look back at page 26. Use details from the selection in your answer.

Meet author **and** illustrator
Christopher Myers on page 421.

Write Now

Poem

Prompt

Wings describes a boy who can fly.
Think about what it would be like to fly.
Now write a poem about flying.

Writing Trait

Many poems are **organized** into lines and stanzas. Often words at the ends of lines rhyme.

Student Model

Where Can You Fly?

I could watch my kite as it dances way up high,
Bright red, yellow, green, bold against the sky.
I could climb to the top of a tall, leafy tree,
Where birds perch before they soar away from me.

On a roller coaster, at the top of the hill,
Zooming down, wind in my face, flying's a thrill!
Flying even higher, I hear only a roaring sound,
Under the wings of a plane, high above the ground.

This poem is <u>organized</u> into two stanzas. Each stanza has four lines.

Rhyming words at ends of lines create rhythm, or a musical pattern.

Vivid words help create pictures in readers' minds.

Use the model to help you write your own poem.

29

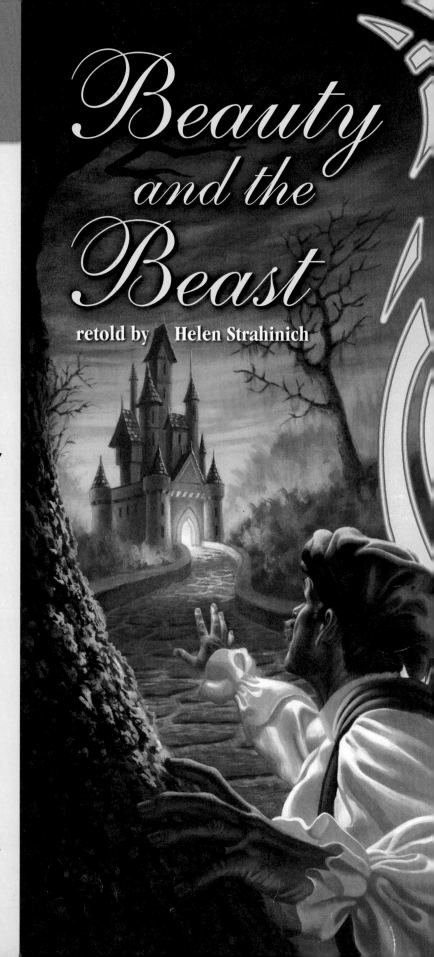

Fairy Tale

Genre

- Fairy tales often have magical characters and events.

- Many fairy tales begin with "Once upon a time . . ." to show that the story takes place long ago and far away.

- Many fairy tales end with "they lived happily ever after" to indicate a happy ending.

Link to Reading

Look for other fairy tales in the library. Try to find different versions of the same tale. Read and compare the versions. Discuss them with your classmates.

Beauty
and the
Beast

retold by   Helen Strahinich

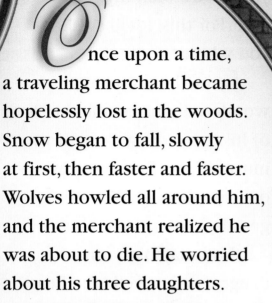

Once upon a time, a traveling merchant became hopelessly lost in the woods. Snow began to fall, slowly at first, then faster and faster. Wolves howled all around him, and the merchant realized he was about to die. He worried about his three daughters.

Suddenly, the merchant saw a light in the distance. He walked toward it and soon came upon a castle. He knocked on the door, but no one answered. He entered the castle.

The merchant found himself in a large, splendid room. A fire burned in the fireplace and a luscious feast rested on the table. He waited patiently. No one came, so he ate heartily and fell asleep near the fire.

The next morning, the merchant found fresh clothing by the hearth and breakfast on the table. He waited again, but no one came. So he ate and then went outside.

Cause and Effect   Why was the merchant lost?

The snow had vanished overnight. In the castle courtyard, the merchant saw a rosebush. He plucked one rose for his youngest daughter, named Beauty.

Just then, a heart-stopping roar boomed across the courtyard, and a giant beast galloped toward the merchant. The creature blocked the merchant's path, raising its long, sharp claws. Its mouth was a dark, gruesome cave. Its teeth were fearsome knives. "I showed you kindness," the Beast roared, "and in return, you have stolen my precious rose. For this, I will swallow you whole."

Again, the merchant wondered what would become of his three daughters. "If you must kill me, first grant me one simple wish. Let me say goodbye to my daughters."

"You may bid your daughters farewell," the Beast told him, "and if one of them will take your place, then you may go free."

The merchant returned home and told his three daughters about these terrifying events. The oldest daughters wept, but Beauty begged to take her father's place. Later, father and daughter returned to the castle. The merchant pleaded with the Beast to let him stay with Beauty, but the Beast sent him away.

Beauty was sure that the Beast would devour her. Instead, he spent much time with her and treated her like a princess. Beauty was in want of nothing. Each night the Beast requested Beauty's hand in marriage, and each night she refused, for she was repelled by his beastly looks.

However, Beauty's feelings changed little by little. Soon the Beast's appearance became less important. Beauty began to appreciate his gentleness and kindness. She saw his inner beauty and looked forward to visiting with the Beast each night.

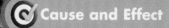 **Cause and Effect**   What caused the Beast to become angry with the merchant?

Still, Beauty missed her father deeply. "If you will allow me to visit my father, I will promise to marry you when I return."

"You may go, but if you do not return in one week, I will die of sadness." The Beast gave her a magic ring that would return her to the castle in an instant.

The merchant was delighted to see Beauty safe, happy, and well taken care of. Her older sisters were jealous, however, and they tricked her into staying beyond the week's deadline.

One night Beauty awoke crying. She had dreamed that the Beast was dying in his garden, clutching his heart. Quickly she put on the magic ring. In a breath, she found herself in the castle garden.

Beauty ran to the dying Beast and cried, "I love you, and I want to marry you."

Beauty's words and tears were like medicine for the Beast. Suddenly, the castle fireworks glowed and music played. When Beauty looked again, she saw that the Beast had disappeared and, in his place, was a handsome prince.

"Your kindness saved me from a spell," the prince explained. "I was turned into a beast, and I had to stay a beast until a kind-hearted girl agreed to marry me."

Beauty married her prince, and they lived happily ever after.

Reading Across Texts
How are the main characters in *Wings* and "Beauty and the Beast" alike and different?

Writing Across Texts Make a chart. Compare and contrast the main characters in the two selections.

Answer Questions What saved the prince? Where will you find the answer?

Compare and Contrast

- When you compare and contrast, you tell how things are alike and different.

- When you read, look for clue words that signal comparisons and contrasts, such as *like*, *both*, *different*, and *however*.

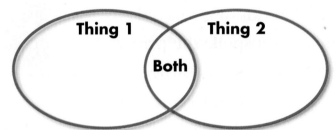

 ## Strategy: Ask Questions

Good readers ask themselves questions when they read. Doing this will give you a purpose for reading. As you read, you might ask yourself, "How are these things alike? How are they different? What do I already know about these things?"

Write to Read

1. Read "The Two Largest U.S. Cities." Make a Venn diagram like the one above. Write New York City and Los Angeles as headings. Write Both in the middle. Fill in the diagram.

2. Write a question that calls for comparing the two cities. Use your completed diagram to answer the question.

The Two Largest U.S. Cities

Which city do you think is the largest in the United States? If you guessed New York City, you are correct. More than 7 million people live there!

Los Angeles, California, is the second largest city in the United States. More than 3 million people live in Los Angeles.

New York City is on the East Coast. It lies mostly on islands in a harbor. Los Angeles is on the West Coast of the country. It has the Pacific Ocean on one side of the city and mountains on the other.

The weather in New York City is very different from the weather in Los Angeles. New York City has cold winters with snow. It has warm summers. However, Los Angeles has mild weather all year long.

Many people from other countries live in both New York City and Los Angeles. Which large city would you like to visit?

Strategy: How does this information compare with what you already know about New York City or Los Angeles? Ask yourself, "What else might be alike and different about these two cities?"

Skill: Which clue words signal a contrast in this paragraph?

37

Vocabulary Strategy
for Compound Words

Word Structure When you are reading, you may come across a long word that looks like two words. Look closely at the word. Do you see two small words in it? It may be a compound word. You may be able to use the two small words to help you figure out the meaning of the compound word. For example, *rainfall* is the amount of rain that falls at any one time.

1. Divide the compound word into its two small words.

2. Think of the meaning of each small word, and put the two meanings together.

3. Try the new meaning in the sentence. Does it make sense?

Read "Geography Bee." Use the meanings of the two small words in each compound word to help you figure out the meaning of the compound word.

GEOGRAPHY BEE

Have you heard of a geography bee? You probably know what a spelling bee is. In a spelling bee, people take turns spelling difficult words. The person who spells the most words correctly wins. In a geography bee, people answer questions about places on Earth.

The questions in a geography bee will never have a yes or no answer. For example, this question would not be used in a geography bee: Can a person outrun the tides at the Bay of Fundy?

To answer the questions in a geography bee, you must know facts about continents, countries, states, and physical features of the world, such as deserts or oceans.

Here are some sample questions for you to try: What is the hottest spot on Earth? Which is the highest of all the waterfalls on Earth? Which mountain peak is the tallest in the world? What is the average summer temperature at the South Pole? What is the depth of the Marianas Trench?

Do you know the answer to these questions? Perhaps you will soon find out.

Words to Write

Look at the pictures in *Hottest, Coldest, Highest, Deepest,* and read the captions. Write four questions that could be used in a geography bee. Then write the answers. Use words from the Words to Know list.

HOTTEST
COLDEST
HIGHEST
DEEPEST

BY STEVE JENKINS

Genre

Expository nonfiction gives information about the real world. Look for numbers and diagrams that help you understand the facts.

How does the environment where you
live compare to these extreme locations?

I f you could visit any spot on Earth, where would you go? What if you wanted to see some of the most amazing natural wonders in the world?

There are deserts that haven't seen rain for hundreds of years and jungles where it pours almost every day. There are places so cold that even in the summer it's below freezing and spots where it's often hot enough to cook an egg on the ground. There are mountains many miles high and ocean trenches that are even deeper. You can find rivers thousands of miles long and waterfalls thousands of feet high.

Where are the very hottest and coldest, windiest and snowiest, highest and deepest places on Earth? Travel the world and visit the planet's record holders.

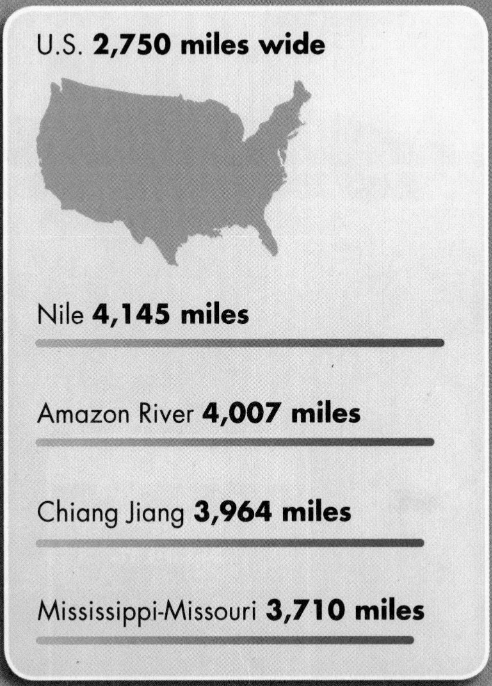

U.S. **2,750 miles wide**

Nile **4,145 miles**

Amazon River **4,007 miles**

Chiang Jiang **3,964 miles**

Mississippi-Missouri **3,710 miles**

The Nile, in Africa, is the **longest** river in the world. It is 4,145 miles long.

The Amazon River, in South America, is not as long—4,007 miles—but it is considered mightier because it carries half of all the river water in the world. The Chiang Jiang (Yangtze), in Asia (3,964 miles), and the Mississippi–Missouri, in the United States (3,710 miles), are the world's third and fourth longest rivers.

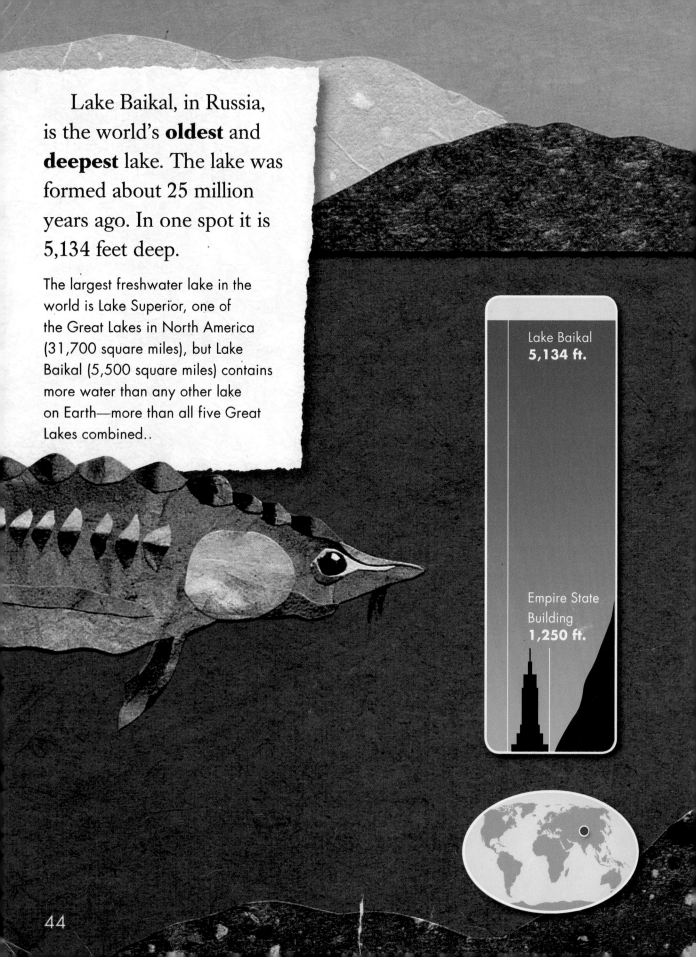

Lake Baikal, in Russia, is the world's **oldest** and **deepest** lake. The lake was formed about 25 million years ago. In one spot it is 5,134 feet deep.

The largest freshwater lake in the world is Lake Superior, one of the Great Lakes in North America (31,700 square miles), but Lake Baikal (5,500 square miles) contains more water than any other lake on Earth—more than all five Great Lakes combined..

Lake Baikal
5,134 ft.

Empire State Building
1,250 ft.

Mount Everest is the **highest** mountain in the world. Its peak is 29,028 feet above sea level.

Mount Everest is considered the **highest** mountain—above sea level—in the world, but it's not really the **tallest.** Measured from its base on the floor of the ocean, Mauna Kea, in Hawaii, is 33,476 feet tall. Only the top 13,796 feet of Mauna Kea are above sea level.

The **hottest** spot on the planet is Al Aziziyah, Libya, in the Sahara, where a temperature of over 136°F has been recorded.

The hottest temperature ever recorded in the United States is 134.6°F, in Death Valley, California.

136°F
134.6°F

98.6°F
Body temp.

68°F
Room temp.

32°F
Water freezes

The **coldest** place on the planet is Vostok, Antarctica. A temperature of 129°F below zero was recorded there.

It is so cold at the South Pole that the average summer temperature is –58°F. The coldest temperature ever recorded in the United States is –80°F, at Prospect Creek Camp, Alaska.

The **wettest** place on Earth is Tutunendo, Colombia, where an average of 463 inches of rain falls every year.

Mount Wai-ale-ale, on the island of Kauai in Hawaii, has the most rainy days—350 a year. On the island of La Réunion, in the Indian Ocean, more than 61 inches of rain fell in a single day.

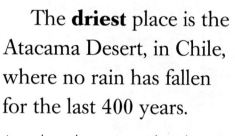

The **driest** place is the Atacama Desert, in Chile, where no rain has fallen for the last 400 years.

Any place that receives less than 10 inches of precipitation a year is considered a desert. The driest place in the United States is Death Valley, California, where only about 1½ inches of rain fall every year.

72 in. Adult man

10 in.
Desert precipitation

1½ in.
Death Valley
average annual
precipitation

The **windiest** spot on Earth is atop Mount Washington, in New Hampshire. A wind speed of 231 miles per hour has been recorded there.

It is also very windy near the tops of the world's highest mountains, the Himalayas. Many of these peaks are tall enough to reach the jet stream, a narrow, strong air current that is found above 28,000 feet.

The world's **highest** waterfall is Angel Falls, in Venezuela. It is 3,212 feet high.

Angel Falls is more than seventeen times higher than Niagara Falls (180 feet), in New York State. Victoria Falls, in Zimbabwe, Africa, carries more water than any other waterfall. It is 355 feet high.

Angel Falls
3,212 ft.

Victoria Falls
355 ft.

Empire State Building
1,250 ft.

Niagra Falls
180 ft.

The **deepest** spot in the ocean is the Marianas Trench, in the Philippines. It is 36,202 feet deep.

The average depth of the world's oceans is about 3 miles, or 16,000 feet. The lowest spot on dry land is the shore of the Dead Sea, 1,100 feet below sea level.

The world's **most active** volcano is Sangay, in Ecuador. Since 1937 it has erupted once every 24 hours on average. It once erupted more than 400 times in a single day.

Other very active volcanoes include Colima, in Mexico (it has erupted regularly since 1560); Aso, in Japan (erupting since 533); and Mount Etna, in Italy (erupting regularly since 1500 B.C.).

51

The **most extreme tides** occur in the Bay of Fundy, in Nova Scotia, Canada. There the water level rises and falls more than 50 feet every 6 hours.

The tide here comes in so fast that it can overtake a person trying to outrun it.

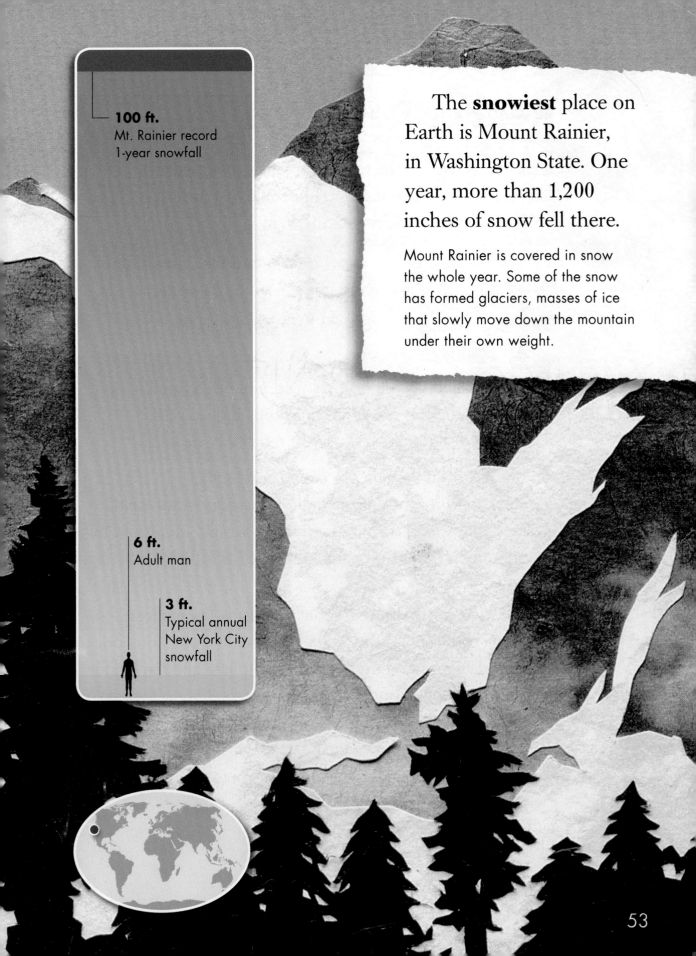

100 ft.
Mt. Rainier record
1-year snowfall

6 ft.
Adult man

3 ft.
Typical annual
New York City
snowfall

The **snowiest** place on Earth is Mount Rainier, in Washington State. One year, more than 1,200 inches of snow fell there.

Mount Rainier is covered in snow the whole year. Some of the snow has formed glaciers, masses of ice that slowly move down the mountain under their own weight.

Reader Response

Open for Discussion Now, after reading *Hottest, Coldest, Highest, Deepest,* if you could visit any spot on Earth, where would you go? Why?

1. Why did the author show a man and the Empire State Building on some of the pages? **Think Like an Author**

2. Compare and contrast the Nile River and the Amazon River. **Compare and Contrast**

3. This selection is full of facts. Did you have trouble reading any parts? What questions did you ask? How did that help you as you read? **Ask Questions**

4. The words in the title are called *superlatives.* This means they stand for the "most" in that category—*hot, cold, high,* and *deep.* Which superlative would you use to talk about cars? chili? a computer game? a toad? **Vocabulary**

Look Back and Write Mount Everest is the highest mountain, but Mauna Kea is the tallest mountain. Look back at page 45. Write the reason that the tallest and the highest are not the same. Use details from the selection to explain your answer.

Meet author **and illustrator Steve Jenkins on page 416.**

Write Now

Describe a Setting

Prompt

Hottest, Coldest, Highest, Deepest describes interesting places around the world.

Think about an interesting or unusual place you know.

Now write a description of that place, using vivid words.

First sentence identifies the place that will be described.

Details are organized in time order.

Word choice appeals to readers' senses of sight, hearing, smell, touch, and taste.

Student Model

We had a wonderful time at Camp Big Timber. In the morning, our happy shouts filled the air as we splashed in the cool, refreshing water of the deep pool. In the afternoon, our colorful sailboats bobbed on the lapping waves of the lake. Each day ended with the smoky smell of a crackling campfire and the taste of gooey, melted marshmallows. Tiny points of bright light glittered in the black sky above.

Use the model to help you write a description of a setting.

Picture Encyclopedia

Genre

- Picture encyclopedias provide information about many topics.

- They include photos with captions.

Text Features

- The photographs and captions in this article compare very large and very small animals.

- You can read captions left to right or top to bottom. If you prefer, you can even skip around.

Link to Science

Choose two animals not described in this article. Use reference sources to find out about them. Draw pictures and write captions to compare the animals.

Great
and Small

from *Factastic Book of Comparisons*
by Russell Ash

Animals come in every shape imaginable. But who tops the charts when it comes to size? Check out these incredible animal comparisons and see why they are in a class of their own!

Twice as tall as all the rest

The giraffe is by far the tallest animal. It is up to twice as tall as the African elephant and more than three times as tall as the average man. Its long legs and long neck allow it to browse on treetop leaves beyond the reach of even an elephant's long trunk.

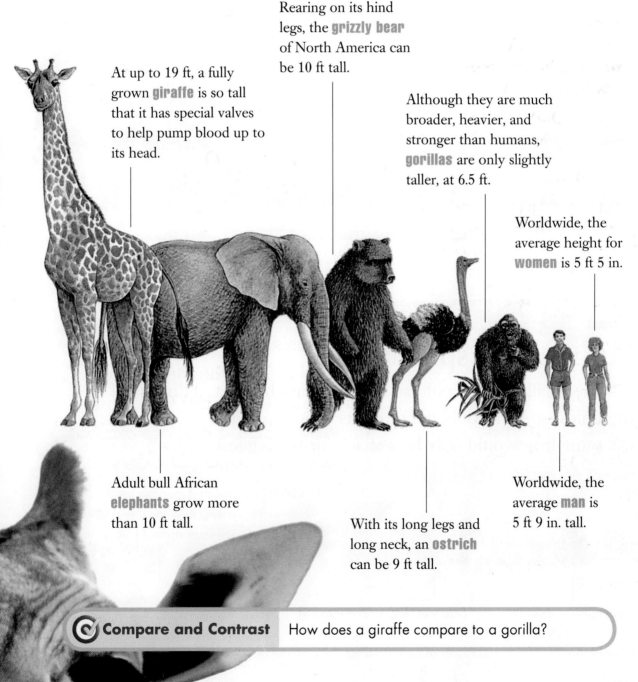

Rearing on its hind legs, the grizzly bear of North America can be 10 ft tall.

At up to 19 ft, a fully grown giraffe is so tall that it has special valves to help pump blood up to its head.

Although they are much broader, heavier, and stronger than humans, gorillas are only slightly taller, at 6.5 ft.

Worldwide, the average height for women is 5 ft 5 in.

Adult bull African elephants grow more than 10 ft tall.

With its long legs and long neck, an ostrich can be 9 ft tall.

Worldwide, the average man is 5 ft 9 in. tall.

Compare and Contrast How does a giraffe compare to a gorilla?

Long-gone Jurassic giant

The biggest dinosaurs were plant eaters. They were bigger than any living land animals because they had no competitors. One of the longest, measured from nose to tail tip, was *diplodocus,* which lived on the North American continent some 145 million years ago. *Diplodocus* was nearly three times as long as the longest land animal living today, the reticulated python.

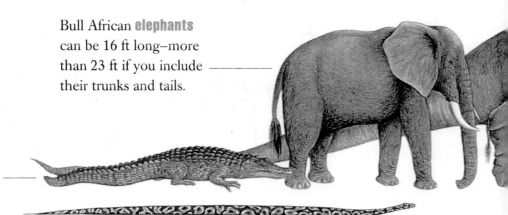

Bull African **elephants** can be 16 ft long–more than 23 ft if you include their trunks and tails.

The Nile **crocodile** grows up to 16 ft in length–more than 125 times as long as the world's smallest gecko.

Found in Asia, and growing up to 35 ft – almost half the length of a tennis court–the reticulated **python** is the longest snake in the world.

Stupendous spider

The smallest frog could sit on your thumbnail–and dozens of the tiniest spiders could dance on its head. Were it not poisonous, the same frog would only be a snack for the biggest spider.

South American bird-eating **spider** (actual size): leg span up to 11 in.

Cuban arrow-poison **frog** (actual size): only 0.5 in. long

Patu marplesi, a **spider** found in Western Samoa, has a leg span of only 0.017 in.

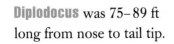 Diplodocus was 75–89 ft long from nose to tail tip.

A dromedary camel can be 10 ft long from the end of its nose to the base of its tail.

A tiger can be 9 ft long– about six times as long as a domestic cat.

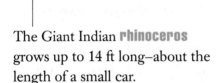

The Giant Indian rhinoceros grows up to 14 ft long–about the length of a small car.

Zebras can grow up to 7.5 ft long.

Reading Across Texts

You have read about the hottest, coldest, highest, deepest places on Earth and about the biggest and smallest creatures on Earth. Is it important to keep track of these facts?

Writing Across Texts Write a paragraph explaining your answer.

Compare and Contrast How do arrow-poison frogs compare to other frogs?

Skill
Generalize

Strategy
Prior Knowledge

 Skill

Generalize

- When you read, you can sometimes make a general statement about what you have read.

- A general statement tells how some things are mostly alike or all alike.

- Look for examples. Ask what they have in common.

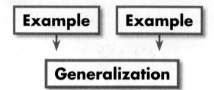

```
Example        Example
     |             |
     v             v
      Generalization
```

 Strategy

Strategy: Prior Knowledge

Active readers use what they already know to help them understand what they read. Use what you know and what you read to form a general statement.

Write to Read

1. Read "Looking at Rocks." Make a graphic organizer like the one above. Write examples that tell about different rocks. Then write a general statement about what rocks are made of.

2. Write one thing you already knew about rocks that helped you make your general statement.

LOOKING AT ROCKS

Have you ever looked at rocks? Some rocks look the same all over. They are made of one thing. However, most rocks do not look the same all over. Some have different colors. Some have sparkles. Others have shiny spots. The colors and sparkles and shines come from the different materials mixed together in the rock.

If you like looking at rocks, you can get a job working with rocks when you grow up. Some scientists look at rocks to find out about dinosaurs from long ago. Other scientists look at rocks to find oil. Some rock scientists help builders make safe buildings. Others try to predict when an earthquake will happen or a volcano will erupt.

Rocks can tell us many things. Take a look!

Strategy: Here's where you can use what you know to help you understand better. Think of rocks you have seen. What do they look like?

Skill: This paragraph tells about different kinds of rocks. What generalization can you make? Ask yourself, "What do most rocks seem to have in common?"

61

stamps

spare

chores

attic

labeled

customer

board

Remember

Try the strategy. Then, if you need more help, use your glossary or a dictionary.

Vocabulary Strategy
for Multiple-Meaning Words

Context Clues Sometimes when you are reading, you may see a word you know but whose meaning doesn't make sense in the sentence. The word may have more than one meaning. For example, *bear* means "a large furry animal," but it also can mean "to carry."

1. Try the meaning of the word that you know. Does it make sense in the sentence?

2. If it doesn't make sense, perhaps it has another meaning. Read on and look at the words around it. Can you figure out another meaning?

3. Try the new meaning in the sentence. Does it make sense?

As you read "More Than a Hobby," look for words that might have more than one meaning. Remember to use nearby words to figure out a new meaning.

More Than a Hobby

It starts out as a hobby. As a child, you collect stamps or toy cars or rocks. At first, collecting is an activity you do in your spare time or after doing your chores.

Perhaps you collect a few rocks here and a few rocks there. Then one day you realize that the shelves in your room are bulging with rocks. So you move them to the basement or the attic where there is more space.

As you get older, you learn more about rocks, and you talk with other rock collectors. You begin to think, "Maybe this isn't just a hobby. Could it be a business?"

So you open a rock shop. Every rock in the shop is labeled, telling all about it and how much it costs. This really impresses your very first customer, so he buys several rocks. You are on your way.

Over time, your small business grows large, and you become the chairman of the board. And all from a hobby.

Words to Write

What kind of shop would you like to open? Write about your shop. Use as many words from the Words to Know list as you can.

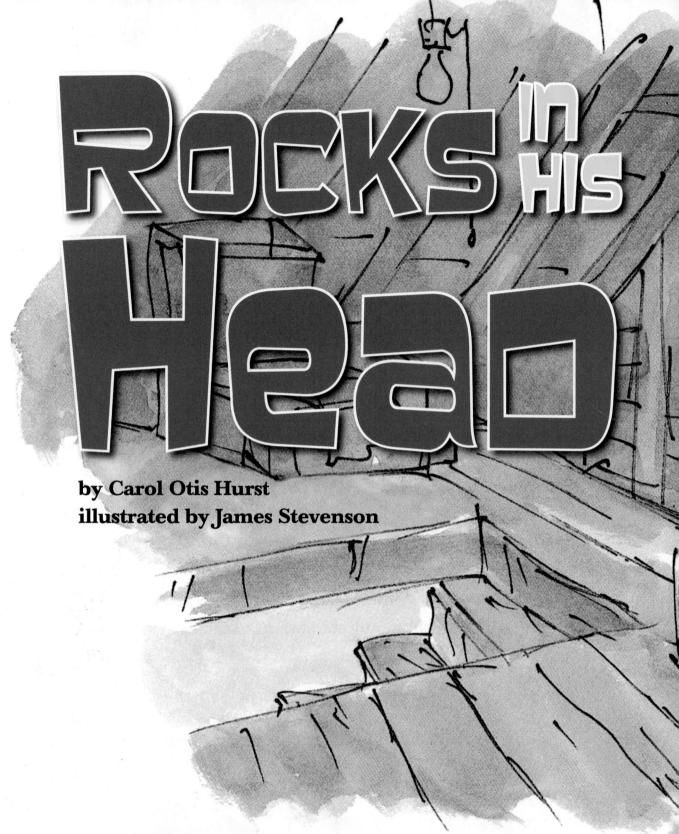

Rocks IN HIS Head

by Carol Otis Hurst

illustrated by James Stevenson

Genre

A **biography** is the story of a real person's life, written by another person. How is this author connected to the person she wrote about?

**Who has rocks in his head, and
what does that mean?**

Some people collect stamps. Some people collect coins or dolls or bottle caps. When he was a boy, my father collected rocks. When he wasn't doing chores at home or learning at school, he'd walk along stone walls and around old quarries, looking for rocks. People said he had rocks in his pockets and rocks in his head. He didn't mind. It was usually true.

When people asked what he wanted to be when he grew up, he'd say, "Something to do with rocks, I think."

"There's no money in rocks," someone said.

"Probably not," said my father.

When he grew up, my father decided to open a gas station. (People called them filling stations then.) My grandfather helped him build one on Armory Street in Springfield, Massachusetts.

They called the station the Antler Filling Station. My father carefully painted the name right over the doorway.

Inside the filling station was a desk with a cash drawer (which my father usually forgot to lock) and a table for his chess set.

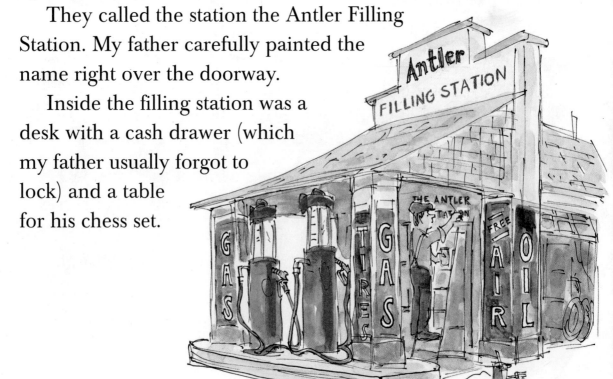

My father built narrow wooden shelves on the back wall and painted them white. People said, "What are those shelves for?"

He said, "I've got rocks in my head, I guess."

Then, one by one, he placed his rocks and minerals on those shelves. He carefully labeled each rock to show what kind it was and where it had come from.

In those days lots of rich people had automobiles, but then Henry Ford came out with the Model T.

That was a car many people could afford. My father had taken one apart and put it back together again and again until he knew every inch of the Model T. He thought that anyone who had spare parts for the Model T and could repair it so that it drove like new would do a good business. He bought some parts from dealers and found some parts in junkyards.

The pile of Model T parts sat just to the left of the lift. Soon, that pile of parts was bigger than the filling station.

People said, "If you think people are going to buy that junk, you've got rocks in your head."

"Maybe I have," he said. "Maybe I have."

But people did come to buy that junk. They came to buy gas, and they came to play chess, and they came to look at the rocks.

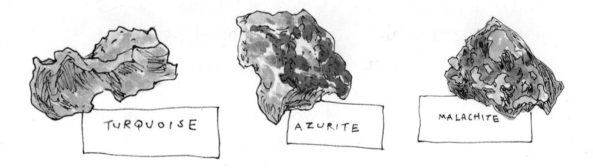

TURQUOISE   AZURITE   MALACHITE

For a while my father was too busy for the chess games. He was pumping gas, changing tires, and fixing Model Ts.

"Where did you get this one?" a customer would say, holding up a rock.

"Found it in a slag pile in New Hampshire," he'd say. Or, "Traded for it with a fella from Nevada. Gave him some garnets from Connecticut."

"People in Nevada and Connecticut collect rocks like you do?" people would ask.

"Lots of folks have rocks in their heads," said my father. He'd dig into his pocket and take out a rock. "Take a look at this one."

Then the stock market fell. At first, people didn't think it would matter much to my father. After all, he had no money in the stock market.

"I may have rocks in my head," he said, "but I think bad times are coming."

And bad times did come. People couldn't afford to buy new cars or fix their old ones.

When business was slow, my father would play chess with some of his customers. When business was very slow, my grandfather would mind the filling station, and we'd pile as many of us kids as would fit into our Model T, and we'd hunt for more rocks with my father.

He had to build more shelves for the rocks, up the west wall of the station.

Then people stopped coming for gas. They stopped coming to play chess, and they even stopped coming to look at the rocks and minerals. They were all too busy looking for work.

One day my father picked up the chess set and carefully packed it in a big box. He took down each mineral, wrapped it in newspaper, and carefully placed it in a wooden box.

When his friends came with a truck to help us move, they said, "Watch out for those wooden boxes. He's got rocks in his boxes, now."

"Yessir," said my father. "That's just what I got in there. Take a look at this one."

The house we moved to was old and falling apart. My father said he'd have it fixed up in no time.

But before he started in on the repairs, we had to take those rocks up to the attic, where he'd already built tiny little wooden shelves.

My father did fix up the old house, and after he finished each repair, he went up to the attic with his rocks. He spent a lot of time reading about rocks, too.

"If you think those rocks are ever going to do you any good," said my mother, "you've got rocks in your head."

"Maybe I have," said my father. "Maybe I have." He reached into his pocket. "Take a look at this one."

My father spent a lot of time looking for any job he could find. Most jobs lasted only a day or two.

On rainy days when my father could find no other work, he'd take the bus to the science museum. They had a whole room full of glass cases containing many rocks. Sometimes he'd spend the whole day in that room.

One afternoon he looked up to see a lady standing beside him. "I've seen you here before," she said.

"I come here a lot," he said. "I guess I've got rocks in my head."

"Tell me what you're looking for," she said.

"I'm looking for rocks that are better than mine," he said.

"How many did you find?" she asked.

"Ten," he said.

The lady looked around at the hundreds of rocks, in all those glass cases. "Only ten?"

"Maybe eleven," he said.

He smiled. She did, too.

"You *have* got rocks in your head," she said. "I'm Grace Johnson, the director of this museum. These rocks have come from all over the world."

"So have mine," said my father. He reached into his pocket. "Take a look at this one," he said.

"Did you study rocks at college?" she asked.

"Couldn't afford to go to college," he said.

"Let me see the rest of your rocks," she said.

Mrs. Johnson got out her big Packard touring car, and my father got in. They drove to our house.

"Where are the rocks?" she asked.

"Up here," said my father, leading the way to the attic. "Watch your step."

Two hours later Mrs. Johnson said, "I can't hire you as a mineralogist. The board won't allow it. But I need a night janitor at the museum. Will you take the job?"

"Will I be cleaning rocks?" he asked.

"Sometimes," she said.

So my father took the job as night janitor at the museum. Before he went home, he'd open some of the mineral cases and scrub some of the rocks with a toothbrush until they sparkled like diamonds.

Mrs. Johnson came in early for work one morning and saw him carefully writing a new label for one of the rocks.

"What are you doing?" she asked.

"One rock was labeled wrong," he said. "I fixed it."

Mrs. Johnson smiled. "I've been talking to the board of directors. They know that I need a person here who knows as much about rocks as you do."

"What about the college education?" he asked.

She said, "I told them I need somebody with rocks in his head and rocks in his pockets. Are you it?"

"Maybe I am," said my father. "Maybe I am."

He reached into his pocket and took out a rock. "Take a look at this one," he said.

Reader Response

Open for Discussion Why did the author's father collect rocks? What do you collect? Why do you think people collect things?

1. The author tells you that her father has rocks in his head. Is she making fun of him? Is she proud of him? How can you tell? **Think Like an Author**

2. What did you learn about collecting things? What would you do with a collection? **Generalize**

3. What do you know about rocks? What do you know about collecting? How did what you know help you as you read? **Prior Knowledge**

4. Make cards with multiple-meaning words from the list and from the story. Work with a partner. Make up a sentence using one of the word's meanings. Ask your partner to tell what the word means in your sentence. **Vocabulary**

Look Back and Write The father collected other things besides rocks. Look back at pages 67–68. Then use information from the selection to write what the father collected and why.

Meet author **Carol Otis Hurst on page 417 and** illustrator **James Stevenson on page 423.**

75

Write Now

Memoir

Prompt

Rocks in His Head describes an important experience in someone's life.

Think about an experience that is important to you.

Now write a memoir about the experience.

Writing Trait

Using different kinds of **sentences** gives writing a natural flow.

Interesting beginning grabs readers' attention.

Asking and answering questions keeps readers involved in writing.

Different kinds and lengths of sentences make writing sound natural.

Student Model

Woof, woof. Fetch! These words rang in my ears. I had "puppy fever." What was the cure? I needed a puppy of my own! I had wanted a dog forever, but first I had to show that I could be responsible. I cleaned my room, did my homework, and washed the dinner dishes. That just wasn't enough. Then my luck changed. My neighbor needed help. Would I walk her dogs after school? Of course, I would! As I took the leashes, I knew this was the chance to really prove myself. I also got to be with dogs!

Use the model to help you write your own memoir.

76

Hints for Writing Sentences

- Use different words to start your sentences. Starting too many sentences with *I, he, she, the,* or *a* can be boring.
- Perk up your writing by adding questions, commands, and exclamations.
- Vary the lengths of sentences.
- Avoid writing long, stringy sentences.
- Short, choppy sentences sometimes can be combined with connecting words.

Genre

- Poems can create a mood for the reader, such as joy, sadness, or fear.

- A poet often uses imagination and humor to entertain the reader.

- Line length, capitalization, punctuation, and headings in this piece of poetry all work together to show that the poet is being playful.

- Read this poem once just to enjoy it. Then read it again and think about the playful choices the poet made and why.

Link to Writing

Write your own rule for picking out a rock.

EVERYBODY NEEDS A ROCK

by Byrd Baylor

illustrated by Franklin Hammond

Everybody
needs
a rock.

I'm sorry for kids
who don't have
a rock
for a friend.

I'm sorry for kids
who only have
TRICYCLES
BICYCLES
HORSES
ELEPHANTS
GOLDFISH
THREE-ROOM PLAYHOUSES
FIRE ENGINES
WIND-UP DRAGONS
AND THINGS LIKE THAT—
if
they don't have
a
rock
for a friend.

That's why
I'm giving them
my own
TEN RULES
for
finding
a
rock . . .

Not
just
any rock.
I mean
a
special
rock
that you find
yourself
and keep
as long as
you can—
maybe
forever.

Prior Knowledge   What do you already know about rocks?

79

If somebody says,
"What's so special
about that rock?"
don't even tell them.
I don't.

Nobody
is supposed
to know
what's special
about
another person's
rock.

All right.
Here
are
the
rules:

Rule Number 1

If you can,
go to a mountain
made out of
nothing but
a hundred million
small
shiny
beautiful
roundish
rocks.

But if you can't,
anyplace will do.
Even an alley.
Even a sandy road.

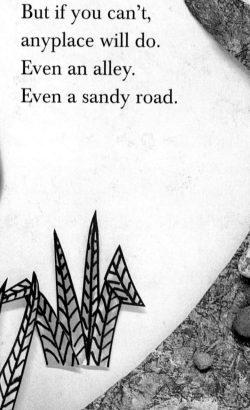

Rule Number 2

When you are looking
at rocks
don't let
mothers or fathers
or sisters or brothers
or even best friends
talk
to you.
You should choose
a rock
when everything
is quiet.
Don't let dogs bark
at you
or bees buzz
at you.

But if they do,
DON'T WORRY.
(The worst thing you can do is go
rock hunting when you are worried.)

Rule Number 3

Bend over.
More.
Even more.
You may have to
sit
on the ground
with your head
almost
touching
the earth.
You have to look
a rock
right
in the eye.

Otherwise,
don't blame me
if you
can't find
a good one.

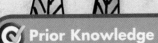 **Prior Knowledge** What do you know that helps you understand Rule 3?

Rule Number 4

Don't get a rock
that is
too big.
You'll
always
be sorry.
It won't fit
your hand
right
and it won't fit
your pocket.

A rock as big as
an apple
is too big.
A rock as big as
a horse
is
MUCH
too big.

Rule Number 5

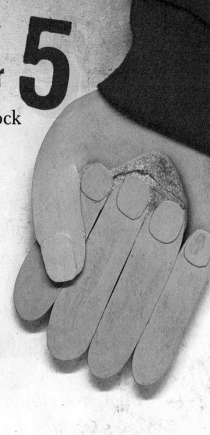

Don't choose a rock
that is
too small.
It will only be
easy
to lose
or
a mouse
might eat it,
thinking
that it
is a seed.

(Believe me,
that happened
to a boy
in the state
of Arizona.)

Rule Number 6

The size
must be
perfect.
It has to feel
easy
in your hand
when you close
your fingers
over it.
It has to feel
jumpy
in your pocket
when you run.

Some people
touch
a rock
a thousand times
a day.
There aren't many things
that feel
as good as a rock–
if the rock
is
perfect.

Rule Number 7

Look for
the perfect
color.
That could be
a sort of
pinkish gray
with bits of
silvery shine in it.
Some rocks
that look brown
are really other
colors,
but
you only see them
when you squint
and when the sun
is right.

Another way
to see colors
is to dip
your rock
in a clear mountain stream–
if one is passing by.

 **Generalize** In general, what can you say about the size of the perfect rock?

Rule Number 8

The shape
of the rock
is up to you.
(There is a girl in Alaska
who only likes flat rocks.
Don't ask me why.
I like them lumpy.)

The thing to remember
about shapes
is this:
Any rock
looks good
with a hundred other rocks
around it on a hill.
But
if your rock
is going to be special
it should look good
by itself
in the bathtub.

Rule Number 9

Always
sniff
a rock.
Rocks have
their own smells.
Some kids can tell
by sniffing
whether a rock
came from the middle
of the earth
or from an ocean
or from a mountain
where wind and sun
touched it
every day
for a million years.

You'll find out that grown-ups
can't tell these things.
Too bad for them.
They just can't smell as well
as kids can.

 **Visualize** Try to create a picture in your mind of the perfect rock.

Rule Number 10

Don't ask anybody
to help you choose.

I've seen
a lizard
pick one rock
out of
a desert full
of rocks
and go sit there
alone.
I've seen
a snail
pass up
twenty rocks
and spend all day
getting to
the one
it wanted.

You have to
make up
your own mind.
You'll
know.

All right,
that's
ten rules.
If you think
of any more
write them down
yourself.
I'm going out
to play a game
that takes
just me
and one rock
to play.

I happen to have
a rock here in my hand. . . .

Reading Across Texts

What do you think the rock collector in *Rocks in His Head* would think of the ten rules in "Everybody Needs a Rock"?

Writing Across Texts Which rule do you think the rock collector would think is most important? Write some sentences telling why you think that.

Comprehension

Skill
Fact and Opinion

Strategy
Monitor and
Fix Up

 Skill

Fact and Opinion

- A statement of fact tells something that can be proved true or false. You can prove it by reading or asking an expert.

- A statement of opinion tells someone's ideas or feelings. Words that tell feelings, such as *should* or *best,* are clues to opinions.

Fact	How to Prove

Opinion	Clue Words

 Strategy

Strategy: Monitor and Fix Up

Sometimes you may be confused by facts that you do not understand. Asking an expert whether a statement of fact is true might help. You can also use a good reference book, such as an encyclopedia.

Write to Read

1. Read "Swim!" Make a chart like the one above. Write two statements of fact and two statements of opinion that you read.

2. Choose one fact from your chart. Use a reference to prove it true or false. Write the reference and what you learned from it.

Swim!

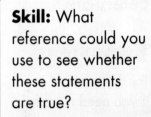

Exercise is important for good health. When people do not exercise, their muscles become soft and weak.

Swimming is one of the best ways to exercise. When swimming, you must move against the water. This makes muscles stronger. It takes more energy to move through water than it does through air. So swimming helps people lose fat. All this also helps your heart get and stay strong.

Skill: What reference could you use to see whether these statements are true?

Many people get hurt playing soccer, football, or basketball. Not in swimming! It's one of the safest ways to exercise.

Swimming is also a great way to have fun while you exercise. You can cool off on a hot summer day and play water games with your friends. Swimming races are an exciting way to beat the heat.

Strategy: This sounds like an opinion. Do you agree? What makes you think so?

If you do not know how to swim, you should learn how—now!

drowned

strokes

medals

current

continued

stirred

celebrate

Remember

Try the strategy. Then, if you need more help, use your glossary or a dictionary.

Vocabulary Strategy
for Multiple-Meaning Words

Context Clues Sometimes when you are reading, you may see a familiar word that doesn't make sense in the sentence. Perhaps the word has another meaning. For example, *bank* means "a place where money is kept," but it also can mean "the ground along a river." Which meaning does *bank* have in this sentence? *We found rocks in the mud on the bank.*

1. Try the meaning of the word that you know. Does it make sense in the sentence?

2. If not, perhaps the word has another meaning. Read on and look at the words around it. Can you figure out another meaning?

3. Try that meaning in the sentence. Does it make sense?

As you read "Learn to Swim," look for words that can have more than one meaning. Use nearby words to figure out a new meaning.

LEARN TO SWIM

Some people swim for exercise, some swim in races, and some swim for fun. But no matter the reason, everyone should learn how to swim. People have drowned because they couldn't swim.

The first step is to learn to float, bob, and tread water. Then learn to swim the basic strokes—front crawl, backstroke, breaststroke, and sidestroke. These are different ways of moving through the water quickly.

Take your time when you're learning to swim. You're not trying to win medals in the Olympics. You do want to coordinate your arms, legs, and breathing.

Even after you know how to swim, never swim where there is no lifeguard. Ocean tides can pull you under, a river's current can sweep you away, and weather can cause problems too. One swimmer continued to swim after it started to rain. High winds stirred up the water. Luckily a boater helped the swimmer back to shore.

So, celebrate the beginning of your life-long swimming adventure. Everyone into the pool!

Words to Write

Write about another sport or activity you know. Mention some safety rules for the activity. Use words from the Words to Know list.

89

AMERICA'S CHAMPION SWIMMER:

Gertrude Ederle

by David A. Adler
illustrated by Terry Widener

Genre

A **biography** gives facts about a real person's life. Why did the author write a biography about Gertrude Ederle?

How did Gertrude Ederle surprise the world?

In 1906 women were kept out of many clubs and restaurants. In most states they were not allowed to vote. Many people felt a woman's place was in the home.

But Gertrude Ederle's place was in the water.

Gertrude Ederle was born on October 23, 1906. She was the third of six children and was raised in New York City, where she lived in an apartment next to her father's butcher shop. Her family called her Gertie. Most everyone else called her Trudy.

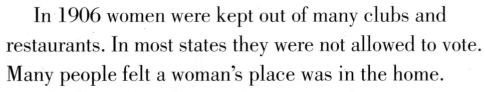

Trudy spent her early years playing on the sidewalks of New York. It wasn't until she was seven that she had her first adventure in the water. While visiting her grandmother in Germany, Trudy fell into a pond and nearly drowned.

After that near disaster, Trudy's father was determined to teach her to swim. For her first lesson, he tied one end of a rope to Trudy's waist and held on to the other end. He put Trudy into a river and told her to paddle like a dog.

Trudy mastered the dog paddle. She joined her older sister Margaret and the other children in the water and copied their strokes. Soon Trudy swam better than any of them.

From that summer on, it was hard to keep Trudy out of the water. She *loved* to swim. At the age of thirteen she became a member of the New York Women's Swimming Association and took lessons there.

At fifteen Trudy won her first big race.

The next year, she attempted to be the first woman to swim the more than seventeen miles from lower Manhattan to Sandy Hook, New Jersey. When Trudy slowed down, her sister Margaret yelled, "Get going, lazybones!" And Trudy did. She finished in just over seven hours. And she beat the men's record.

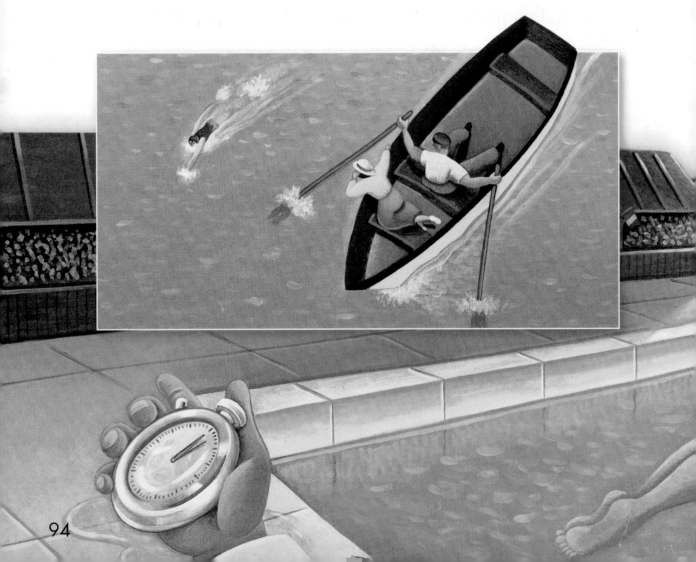

People were beginning to notice Gertrude Ederle. Newspapers described her as courageous, determined, modest, and poised. They called her the most perfect swimmer. Trudy's mother said she was "just a plain home girl."

In 1924 this "plain home girl" was good enough to make the U.S. Olympic team. Trudy won three medals at the games in Paris. Her team won more points than all the other countries' swimming teams combined.

By 1925 Trudy had set twenty-nine U.S. and world records. She was determined to take on the ultimate challenge: the English Channel. Many had tried to swim the more-than-twenty-mile-wide body of cold, rough water that separates England from France. But only five men—and no women—had ever made it all the way across.

Many people were sure Trudy couldn't do it. A newspaper editorial declared that Trudy wouldn't make it and that women must admit they would "remain forever the weaker sex."

It didn't matter to Trudy what people said or wrote. She was going to swim the Channel.

Early in the morning on August 18, 1925, Trudy stepped into the water at Cape Gris-Nez, France, the starting point for the swim. For almost nine hours she fought the strong current. Then, when Trudy had less than seven miles to go, her trainer thought she had swallowed too much water and pulled her, crying, from the sea.

Trudy did not give up her dream. She found a new trainer, and a year later, on Friday, August 6, 1926, she was ready to try again.

Trudy wore a red bathing cap and a two-piece bathing suit and goggles that she and her sister Margaret had designed. To protect her from the icy cold water, Margaret coated Trudy with lanolin and heavy grease. The greasing took a long time—too long for Trudy. "For heaven's sake," she complained. "Let's get started."

Finally, at a little past seven in the morning, she stepped into the water. "Gee, but it's cold," Trudy said.

Trudy's father, her sister Margaret, her trainer, and a few other swimmers were on board a tugboat named *Alsace.* The boat would accompany Trudy to make sure she didn't get lost in the fog and was safe from jellyfish, sharks, and the Channel's powerful currents. There was a second boat, too, with reporters and photographers on board.

As the *Alsace* bobbed up and down in the choppy water, Margaret wrote in chalk on the side of the boat, "This way, Ole Kid." She drew an arrow that pointed to England.

To entertain Trudy, Margaret and some of the others sang American songs, including "The Star-Spangled Banner" and "East Side, West Side." Trudy said the songs kept her "brain and spirit good."

At first the sea was calm.

Trudy swam so fast that her trainer was afraid she would tire herself out. He ordered her to slow down.

Trudy refused.

At about ten-thirty in the morning, Trudy had her first meal. She floated on her back and ate chicken and drank beef broth. A while later, she ate chocolate and chewed on sugar cubes. Then she swam on.

At about one-thirty in the afternoon, it started to rain. A strong wind stirred the water. For a while, Trudy would swim forward a few feet only to be pulled back twice as far.

By six o'clock the tide was stronger. The waves were twenty feet high. The rough water made the people aboard the *Alsace* and the news boat seasick.

Trudy's trainer was sure she couldn't finish the swim. He told her to give up.

"No, no," Trudy yelled over the sound of the waves. She kept swimming.

In the next few hours, the rain and wind became stronger and the sea rougher. At times the rough water pulled the boats away, out of Trudy's sight. She was scared. It was eerie being out there all alone.

Now Trudy began to have trouble kicking in the water. When the *Alsace* came close again, Trudy said her left leg had become stiff. Her trainer was frightened for her. He yelled, "You must come out."

"What for?" Trudy shouted, and kept swimming.

Trudy continued to fight the tide and the constant stinging spray of water in her face. She knew she would either swim the Channel or drown.

As Trudy neared Kingsdown, on the coast of England, she saw thousands of people gathered to greet her. They lit flares to guide her to shore.

At about nine-forty at night, after more than fourteen hours in the water, Trudy's feet touched land. Hundreds of people, fully dressed, waded into the water to greet her. When she reached the shore, her father hugged Trudy and wrapped her in a warm robe.

"I knew if it could be done, it had to be done, and I did it," Trudy said after she got ashore. "All the women of the world will celebrate."

Trudy swam the Channel in just fourteen hours and thirty-one minutes. She beat the men's record by almost two hours. In newspapers across the world, Trudy's swim was called history making. Reporters declared that the myth that women are the weaker sex was "shattered and shattered forever."

Trudy sailed home aboard the SS *Berengaria.* After six days at sea, the ship entered New York Harbor.

Two airplanes circled and tipped their wings to greet Trudy. People on boats of all kinds rang their bells and tooted their horns to salute her. Foghorns sounded.

Trudy climbed into an open car for a parade up lower Broadway. An estimated two million people, many of them women, stood and cheered. They threw scraps of newspaper, ticker tape, pages torn from telephone books, and rolls of toilet paper.

When her car arrived at the New York city hall, Mayor Jimmy Walker praised Trudy for her courage, grace, and athletic prowess. "American women," he said, "have ever added to the glory of our nation."

President Calvin Coolidge sent a message that was read at the ceremony. He called Trudy "America's Best Girl." And she was. Gertrude Ederle had become a beacon of strength to girls and women everywhere.

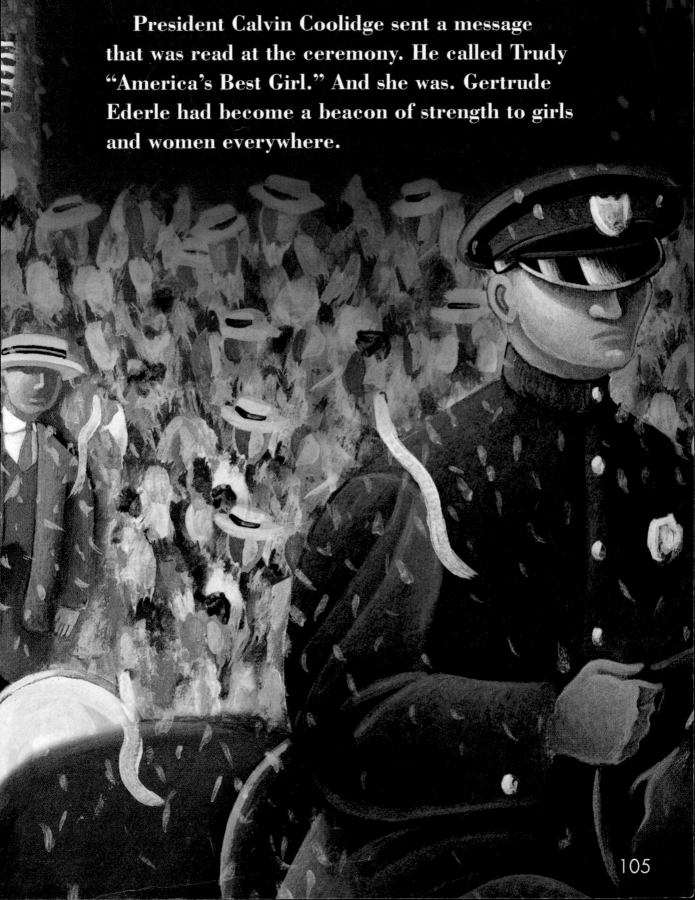

Reader Response

Open for Discussion The English Channel is not like a swimming pool! Imagine you are Trudy, the famous swimmer. As Trudy, explain the difference.

1. David Adler writes many biographies. Many people read them. Why? Look back at this biography. Figure out why it was written and why it is read. **Think Like an Author**

2. This selection is full of facts. Find some. Then find some statements of opinion. Write a sentence that tells your opinion of this selection. **Fact and Opinion**

3. Did anything confuse you as you read this selection? Did you ask someone for help? What reference sources might you go to for help? **Monitor and Fix Up**

4. Think of all the words people used to describe Gertrude Ederle. Make a poster celebrating her success. Decorate it with words from the list and from the selection. **Vocabulary**

Look Back and Write What kind of person was Gertrude Ederle? Look back at page 95. Use details from the selection to tell about Trudy and what she was like.

Meet author David Adler on page 417.

Write Now

Describe a Goal

Prompt

America's Champion Swimmer describes how Gertrude Ederle reached her goal of swimming across the English Channel. Think about a goal you have reached or you want to reach.

Now write a description of that goal.

Student Model

Question at beginning draws readers into writing.

Do you want to be a famous writer? I do! Our school has a Writing Festival each year. It was my chance to be famous. I wanted to write an essay that readers would love, but I was stuck. What should I write about? Writing an essay was like climbing a tall mountain. That was it! I wrote an essay about reaching a goal, and I compared it to climbing a tall mountain. When I was chosen to read my essay at the festival, it felt wonderful—like standing on the top of a tall mountain after a long, hard climb.

"Talking" to readers gives writing a friendly voice.

Image at end neatly returns to subject of essay.

Use the model to help you write your own description of a goal.

Reading Online

New Literacies: **PearsonSuccessNet.com**

Online Directories

Genre

- Online directories group Web sites by topic.

- You can use an online directory or a search engine to find Web sites.

Text features

- Online directories list topics as links on their home page. You may click on any topic link.

- Next, you'll see a list of Web site links on that topic.

Link to Social Studies

Use the library or the Internet to find more information about women athletes. Make a poster to display your information.

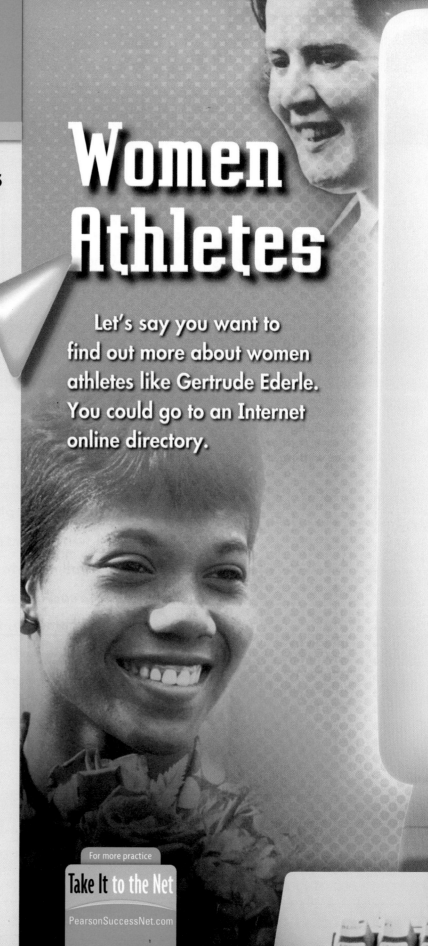

Women Athletes

Let's say you want to find out more about women athletes like Gertrude Ederle. You could go to an Internet online directory.

For more practice

Take It to the Net

PearsonSuccessNet.com

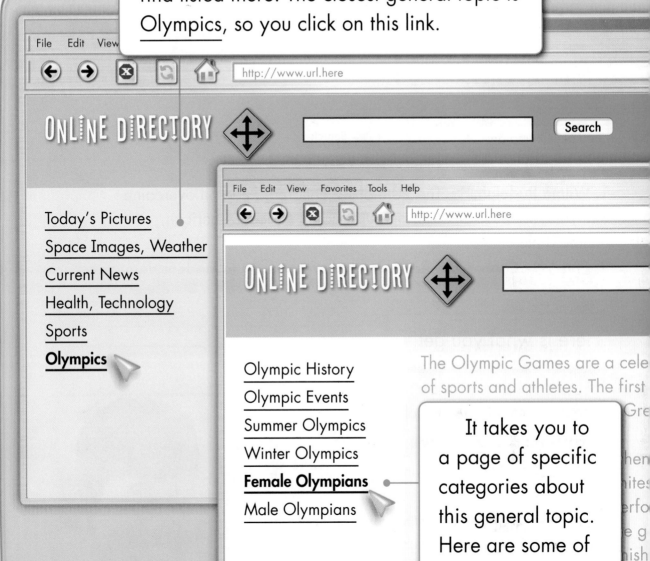

Here are some of the topics you might find listed there. The closest general topic is Olympics, so you click on this link.

File   Edit   View

http://www.url.here

ONLINE DIRECTORY   Search

Today's Pictures
Space Images, Weather
Current News
Health, Technology
Sports
Olympics

File   Edit   View   Favorites   Tools   Help

http://www.url.here

ONLINE DIRECTORY

Olympic History
Olympic Events
Summer Olympics
Winter Olympics
Female Olympians
Male Olympians

The Olympic Games are a cele of sports and athletes. The first

It takes you to a page of specific categories about this general topic. Here are some of them. You click on Female Olympians.

Monitor and Fix Up   If you have trouble understanding, ask an expert to help you.

When you click on Female Olympians, you get a list of Web sites. You decide to click on this one:

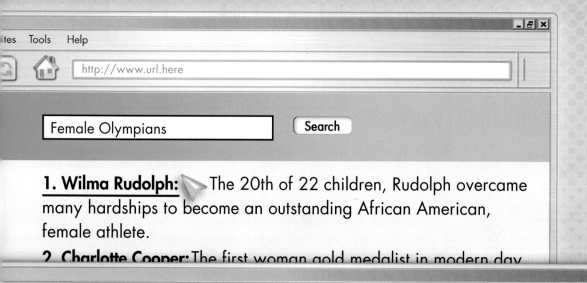

1. **Wilma Rudolph:** The 20th of 22 children, Rudolph overcame many hardships to become an outstanding African American, female athlete.

2. **Charlotte Cooper:** The first woman gold medalist in modern day

Here is what you get.

NAME: Wilma Glodean Rudolph

BIRTHDATE: June 23, 1940

BIRTHPLACE: Clarksville, Tennessee

FAMILY BACKGROUND: Wilma weighed only 4 1/2 pounds when she was born. Because of racial segregation laws, she and her mother were not permitted into the local hospital. Over the next few years, her mother nursed her to health. Then Wilma got polio, a crippling disease that had no cure at the time. The doctor told Mrs. Rudolph that Wilma would never walk. But after hard work, Wilma was finally able to walk with the aid of a metal leg brace. By age 12, she could walk normally. It was then that she decided to become an athlete.

Fact and Opinion Look for facts about Wilma Rudolph that can be proved.

ACHIEVEMENTS: In high school, she became a basketball star. She set state records for scoring. She led her team to a state championship. Then she became a track star, going to her first Olympic Games in 1956. She won a bronze medal in the 4x4 relay.

On September 7, 1960, in Rome, Wilma became the first American woman to win three gold medals in the Olympics. She won the 100-meter dash and the 200-meter dash and ran anchor on the 400-meter relay team.

Reading Across Texts

Think about Gertrude Ederle and Wilma Rudolph. How would you compare the two athletes and their achievements?

Writing Across Texts Write a paragraph comparing the two athletes, and then tell what you think contributed to their exceptional achievements.

111

Comprehension

Skill
Plot and Theme

Strategy
Graphic
Organizers

Plot and Theme

- The plot of a story includes the important things that happen at the beginning, middle, and end.

- As you read, think about what happens in the story and why these things are important.

- As you read, think, "What is the big idea of the story? What did a character learn in this story?"

Strategy: Graphic Organizers

Active readers use graphic organizers to help them see and understand information. You can make a graphic organizer like this one to help you remember the plot as you read.

| Beginning | → | Middle | → | End |

Write to Read

1. Read "Lulu Wants to Grow Up." Note important things that happen in the story.

2. Make a graphic organizer like the one above. List the important things that happened at the beginning, middle, and end of the story.

Lulu Wants to Grow Up

Lulu was a baby eagle, an eaglet. She lived in a nest in the highest branches of the tallest tree high on a mountainside. Lulu did not want to be an eaglet. She wanted to be an eagle. Lulu said, "Tomorrow I will fly."

Mama laughed. "Don't be in such a hurry to grow up! You will fly when you are 12 weeks old. When your feathers change from gray to brown, you can leave the nest."

Skill: You've just read the beginning of the story. What important things have happened so far?

A few days later, Lulu was balancing on the edge of the nest. Suddenly, she slipped. Lulu tumbled down. She got caught on a branch far below.

Slowly, Lulu pulled herself up from branch to branch to the top of the tree. Just then, Mama swooped in from a hunt for food. She grabbed Lulu gently with her claws and dropped her softly into the nest.

Strategy: This ends the middle of the story. What things could you list in a graphic organizer for the beginning and the middle of the story?

Lulu said, "Oh Mama, I don't think I should be in such a hurry to grow up. I'll just stay in our nest until my feathers turn brown and my wings are strong."

"What a smart idea!" Mama said as she hugged Lulu tightly.

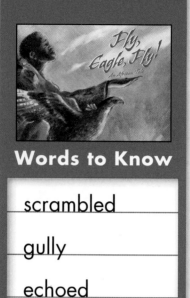

Words to Know

scrambled

gully

echoed

valley

reeds

clutched

Remember

Try the strategy. Then, if you need more help, use your glossary or a dictionary.

Vocabulary Strategy
for Endings

Word Structure Sometimes when you are reading, you may come across a word you don't know. Look closely at the word. Does it have -ed at the end? The ending -ed is usually added to a verb. You may be able to use the ending to help you figure out the meaning of the word.

1. Put your finger over the -ed ending.

2. Look at the base word. Do you know what the base word means?

3. Try your meaning in the sentence. Does it make sense?

As you read "Eagle Watching," look for words that have the -ed ending. Use the ending to help you figure out the meanings of the words.

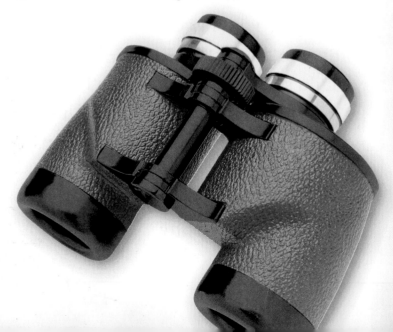

Eagle Watching

José and his father scrambled up the side of the gully. Near the top of the gully was their favorite eagle-watching spot. José and his father looked for the bald eagles that lived in the area. First, they used their binoculars to scan the tops of the trees. Eagles usually perch in high places so that they can look for food. Next, José and his father listened for the eagles. Loud eagle cries often echoed across the valley.

In the valley below where José and his father hid was a large lake. The eagles swooped over the reeds along the lake's edge, skimmed over the surface, and dipped down and snatched a fish out of the water. Then the eagles flew away with the fish clutched in their sharp talons, or claws. They carried the fish back to their nests, high in the tall trees or on the cliffs. It was an amazing sight, and José never got tired of watching it.

Words to Write

Look at this picture. Write about the eagle. What does it look like? What is it doing? Use words from the Words to Know list.

Folk tales are stories or legends from other lands and are handed down from one generation to the next. Where is this story from?

Fly, Eagle, Fly!

An African Tale

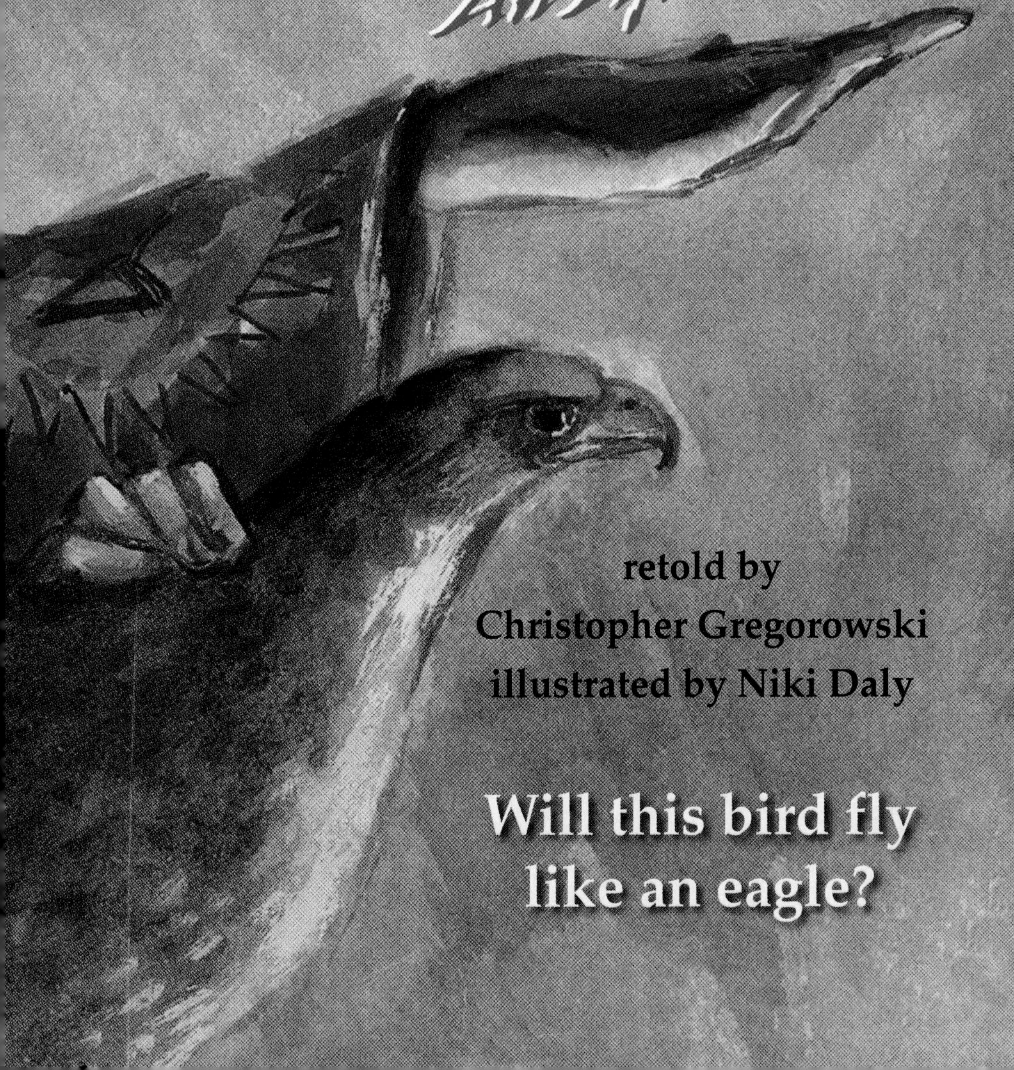

retold by
Christopher Gregorowski
illustrated by Niki Daly

**Will this bird fly
like an eagle?**

A farmer went out one day to search for a lost calf. The little herd boys had come back without it the evening before. And that night there had been a terrible storm.

He went to the valley and searched. He searched by the riverbed. He searched among the reeds, behind the rocks, and in the rushing water.

He wandered over the hillside and through the dark and tangled forests where everything began, then out again along the muddy cattle tracks.

He searched in the long thatch grass, taller than his own head. He climbed the slopes of the high mountain with its rocky cliffs rising to the sky. He called out all the time, hoping that the calf might hear, but also because he felt so alone. His shouts echoed off the cliffs. The river roared in the valley below.

He climbed up a gully in case the calf had huddled there to escape the storm. And that was where he stopped. For there, on a ledge of rock, close enough to touch, he saw the most unusual sight—an eagle chick, very young, hatched from its egg a day or two before and then blown from its nest by the terrible storm.

He reached out and cradled it in both hands. He would take it home and care for it. And home he went, still calling, calling in case the calf might hear.

He was almost home when the children ran out to meet him. "The calf came back by itself!" they shouted. He was very pleased. He showed the eagle chick to his wife and children, then placed it carefully in the warm kitchen among the hens and chicks and under the watchful eye of the roosters.

"The eagle is the king of the birds," he said, "but we shall train it to be a chicken."

So the eagle lived among the chickens, learning their ways. His children called their friends to see the strange bird. For as it grew, living on the bits and pieces put out for the chickens, it began to look quite different from any chicken they had ever seen.

One day a friend dropped in for a visit. He and the
farmer sat at the door of the kitchen hut. The friend
saw the bird among the chickens. "Hey! That's not a
chicken. It's an eagle!"

The farmer smiled at him and said, "Of course it's
a chicken. Look—it walks like a chicken, it talks like a
chicken, it eats like a chicken. It *thinks* like a chicken.
Of course it's a chicken."

But the friend was not convinced. "I will show you
that it is an eagle," he said.

"Go ahead," said the farmer.

The farmer's children helped his friend catch the bird. It was fairly heavy but he lifted it above his head and said: "You are not a chicken but an eagle. You belong not to the earth but to the sky. Fly, Eagle, fly!"

The bird stretched out its wings as the farmer and his family had seen it do before. But it looked about, saw the chickens feeding, and jumped down to scratch with them for food.

"I told you it was a chicken," the farmer said, and roared with laughter.

Next day the friend was back. "Farmer," he said,
"I will prove to you that this is no chicken but an eagle.
Bring me a ladder." With the large bird under one arm,
he struggled up the slippery thatch of the tallest hut.

The farmer doubled over with laughter. "It eats
chicken food. It thinks like a chicken. It *is* a chicken."

The friend, swaying on top of the hut, took the
eagle's head, pointed it to the sky, and said: "You
are not a chicken but an eagle. You belong not
to the earth but to the sky. Fly, Eagle, fly!"

Again the great bird stretched out its wings. It trembled and the claws that clasped his hand opened. "Fly, Eagle, fly!" the man cried.

But the bird scrambled out of his hands, slid down the thatch, and sailed in among the chickens.

There was much laughter.

Very early next morning, on the third day, the farmer's dogs began to bark. A voice was calling outside in the darkness. The farmer ran to the door. It was his friend again. "Give me one more chance with the bird," he begged.

"Do you know the time? It's long before dawn. Are you crazy?"

"Come with me. Fetch the bird."

Reluctantly the farmer went into the kitchen, stepping over his sleeping children, and picked up the bird, which was fast asleep among the chickens. The two men set off, disappearing into the darkness.

"Where are we going?" asked the farmer sleepily.

"To the mountains where you found the bird."

"And why at this ridiculous time of the night?"

"So that our eagle may see the sun rise over the mountain and follow it into the sky where it belongs."

They went into the valley and crossed the river, the friend leading the way. The bird was very heavy and too large to carry comfortably, but the friend insisted on taking it himself.

"Hurry," he said, "or the dawn will arrive before we do!"

The first light crept into the sky as they began to climb the mountain. Below them they could see the river snaking like a long, thin ribbon through the golden grasslands, the forest, and the veld, stretching down toward the sea. The wispy clouds in the sky were pink at first and then began to shimmer with a golden brilliance.

Sometimes their path was dangerous as it clung to the side of the mountain, crossing narrow shelves of rock and taking them into dark crevices and out again. They were both panting, especially the friend who was carrying the bird.

At last he said, "This will do." He looked down the cliff and saw the ground thousands of feet below. They were very near the top.

Carefully the friend carried the bird onto a ledge of rock. He set it down so that it looked toward the east, and began talking to it.

The farmer chuckled. "It talks only chickens' talk."

But the friend talked on, telling the bird about the sun, how it gives life to the world, how it reigns in the heavens, giving light to each new day.

"Look at the sun, Eagle. And when it rises, rise with it. You belong to the sky, not to the earth."

At that moment the sun's first rays shot out over the mountain, and suddenly the world was ablaze with light.

The golden sun rose majestically, dazzling them. The great bird stretched out its wings to greet the sun and feel the life-giving warmth on its feathers. The farmer was quiet. The friend said, "You belong not to the earth, but to the sky. Fly, Eagle, fly!"

He clambered back to the farmer.

All was silent. Nothing moved. The eagle's head stretched up; its wings stretched outwards; its legs leaned forward as its claws clutched the rock.

And then, without really moving, feeling the updraft of a wind more powerful than any man or bird, the great eagle leaned forward and was swept upward, higher and higher, lost to sight in the brightness of the rising sun, never again to live among the chickens.

Reader Response

Open for Discussion A good story needs a good storyteller. Retell *Fly, Eagle, Fly!* so that someone will say, "That's a good story!"

1. *Fly, Eagle, Fly!* has a lesson to teach. What do you think the lesson is? **Think Like an Author**

2. What was the problem in the story, and how was it resolved? **Plot**

3. Make a story map showing what happened at the beginning, the middle, and the end of the story. **Graphic Organizers**

4. The words *gully*, *valley*, and *reeds* describe the land where the farmer searched for his calf. Find other words from the story that also describe the African setting. **Vocabulary**

Look Back and Write What was the farmer's friend's third plan? Look back at page 129. Use information from the selection to write about the third plan and how it worked.

Meet illustrator Niki Daly on page 422.

Write Now

Write About Plot

Prompt

The plot of the African tale *Fly, Eagle, Fly!* is the order in which the events happen. Think about a tale you know well. Now write a summary of the plot of the tale, telling the events in time order.

Writing Trait

As part of your **word choice,** use time-order words and phrases to help readers follow the plot.

First sentence introduces story characters.

Word choice includes time-order words and phrases to make order of events clear.

Last sentence wraps up story by explaining its point.

Student Model

The mighty lumberjack Paul Bunyan had a pet, a giant blue ox named Babe. One day Babe was acting up something awful, so Paul put a rope around Babe's neck and tied the rope to a tree. As soon as Paul went to work, Babe pulled the rope loose and ran off. When Paul came back, he started chasing Babe. They ran all over the state of Minnesota. Everywhere they ran, they left huge footprints. Later, the rains came and filled up the footprints. And that's how Minnesota got 10,000 lakes.

Use the model to help you write your own summary of the plot of a tale.

Purple Coyote

by Cornette
illustrated by Rochette

The coyote did a little dance. Then he balanced himself on his right front paw and let out a strange howl: "WULULI WULA WULILA WUWU WA!"

In the middle of a flat and arid desert stood a hill of sand and rock.

Near this hill was a small house.

Jim played alone in the garden with his old truck, which was missing one wheel.

One day, a coyote appeared on the hill. A coyote unlike any other. A purple coyote.

Jim watched him.

He sat down, letting the evening wind slowly untangle his purple fur.

Night fell and the moon rose. Jim watched the purple coyote until his mother called him for dinner.

Graphic Organizer Make a graphic organizer to keep track of the plot.

The next day, Jim didn't play with his truck, which had lost a second wheel.

He went to wait for the coyote at the bottom of the hill.

The purple coyote appeared. He did his little dance, balanced himself on his right front paw, and let out his "WULULI WULA WULILA WUWU WA!"

Jim climbed up the hill.

It wasn't very hard, as the hill was neither high nor steep.

He went up to the animal, greeted him and asked, "Why are you purple? That's not normal for a coyote!"

"I won't tell you!" answered the coyote.

"Why not?"

"Because it's a secret! But you can ask me questions if you want."

Jim thought hard. He looked the purple coyote

straight in the eyes and asked, "Did you eat too many blueberries?"

"I never eat blueberries," the coyote replied.

Every afternoon, the purple coyote returned to the hill, did his little dance, balanced himself on his front paw, and howled:

"WULULI WULA WULILA WUWU WA!"

Every afternoon, Jim joined the coyote, greeted him, and asked him a question.

"Did you put purple dye on your fur?"

"No," answered the coyote.

"Were you born purple?"

"No."

"Did you catch purple-itis?"

"No."

"Did you catch purple fever?"

"No."

The days went by. Jim began to lose patience.

"I don't care if I never find out why you're purple!" he shouted at the coyote.

 Plot How is the plot developing? Add to your graphic organizer.

In his anger, he thought about not coming up the hill anymore, but his curiosity was too strong.

"Tell me instead why you do that dance and why you howl in that funny way," he asked.

The coyote smiled. "That's my second secret," he said.

Jim tried very hard to keep calm. He acted as though he didn't care. "That's a stupid secret," he said. "Anyone can dance and howl like that! Look!"

Jim did a little dance, then leaned over on his right arm and howled a piercing "WULULI WULA WULILA WUWU WA!"

All at once, Jim turned purple.

As for the coyote, he got his color back. He was once again the color of desert and sand.

"Well done!" said the coyote. "You've discovered my two secrets in one try!

You've given me back my natural color. Now I can leave. Goodbye, Jim!"

He disappeared into the vast desert.

"Yes," said the small animal. "It's my secret," Jim went on. "Do you want to find out why?"

"No."

Jim was now all purple and all by himself.

Night had fallen on the hill when a little raccoon came up to him.

"Hello," the raccoon said.

"Hello!" replied the purple kid.

"Did you see?" said Jim. "I'm purple all over."

Reading Across Texts

Fly, Eagle, Fly! and *Purple Coyote* are both about animals. What makes one story realistic and the other a fantasy?

Writing Across Texts

Make a chart of facts that support your answer.

 Theme What is the big idea of this story? What did Jim learn?

Me

With apologies to Joyce Kilmer ("Trees")

by Karen Jo Shapiro

I think that I will never see,
another person just like me.

Someone who has my color hair,
and picks the kind of clothes I wear.

Someone who thinks the thoughts I think,
and drinks the drinks I like to drink.

Who walks and talks my special way,
and plays the games I choose to play.

So many kinds of folks I see,
but only I can be a ME.

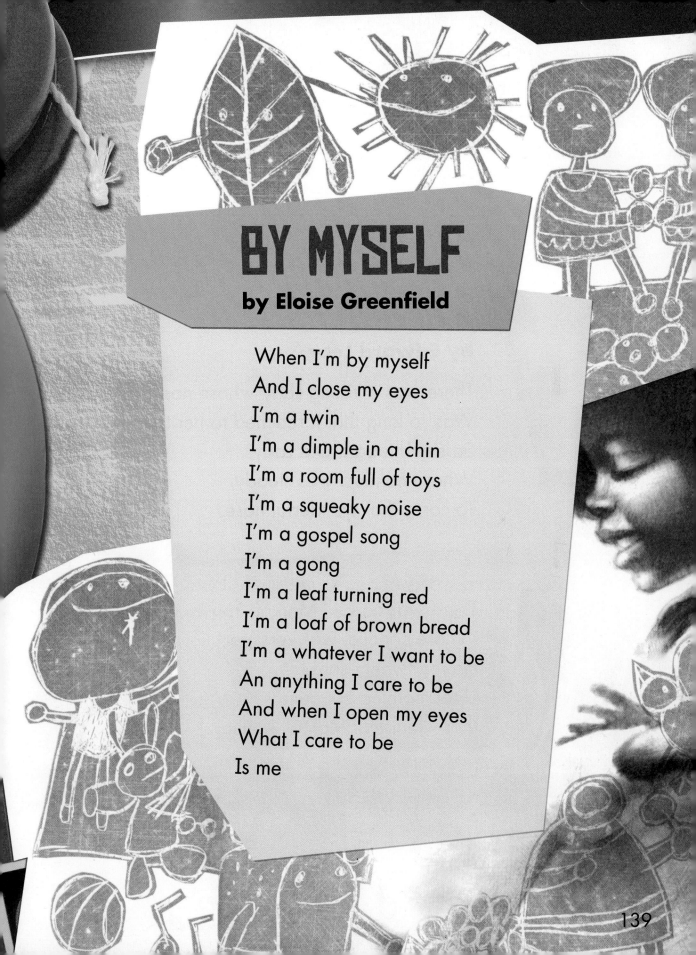

BY MYSELF

by Eloise Greenfield

When I'm by myself
And I close my eyes
I'm a twin
I'm a dimple in a chin
I'm a room full of toys
I'm a squeaky noise
I'm a gospel song
I'm a gong
I'm a leaf turning red
I'm a loaf of brown bread
I'm a whatever I want to be
An anything I care to be
And when I open my eyes
What I care to be
Is me

139

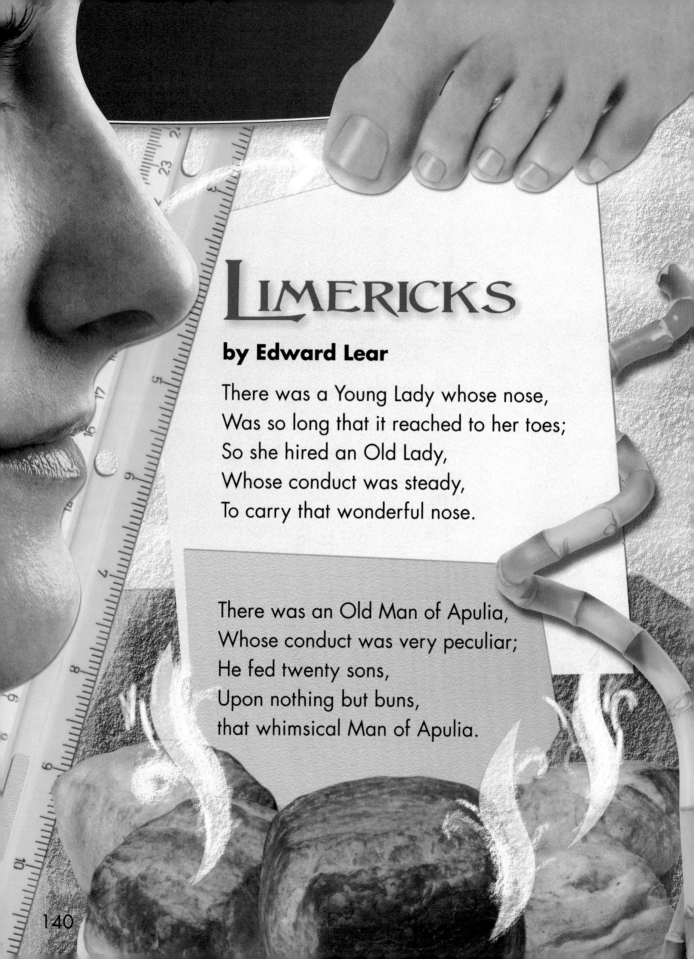

LIMERICKS

by Edward Lear

There was a Young Lady whose nose,
Was so long that it reached to her toes;
So she hired an Old Lady,
Whose conduct was steady,
To carry that wonderful nose.

There was an Old Man of Apulia,
Whose conduct was very peculiar;
He fed twenty sons,
Upon nothing but buns,
that whimsical Man of Apulia.

Written at the Po-Shan Monastery

by Hsin Ch'i-chi
translated by Irving Y. Lo

I would rather be myself:
Why pretend being someone else?
Having traveled everywhere, I've returned
    to farming.
One pine, one bamboo, is a real friend;
Mountain birds, mountain flowers are my
    brothers.

Postcards from a Special Place

connect to
WRITING

Suppose you are visiting one of the unique places you read about in this unit. Write a postcard message that you might send home. In your message, write about what makes the place unique and what you find most impressive. Add a picture to your postcard.

Dear Uncle Vinny,
I'm here at Mt. Everest, the world's tallest mountain!

What does it mean to be unique?

connect to

MATH

Schedule a Visit

You met some unique characters as you read the selections in this unit. Which of these characters would you most like to have as a friend? What would you do if you spent the day together? Make up a schedule for a day with this person. Include some activities that the character would enjoy.

My Day with Ikarus Jackson	
9:00 a.m. — noon	
noon — 2:30 p.m.	
2:30 — 5:00 p.m.	

connect to
SOCIAL
STUDIES

Wonderful, Wonderful Me

You have read about several characters, real and imagined, who are special in some way. What makes you unique? Make yourself a hat, a banner, a medal, or another award that celebrates one way in which you are proud to be unique.

UNIT 5

Read It Online
PearsonSuccessNet.com

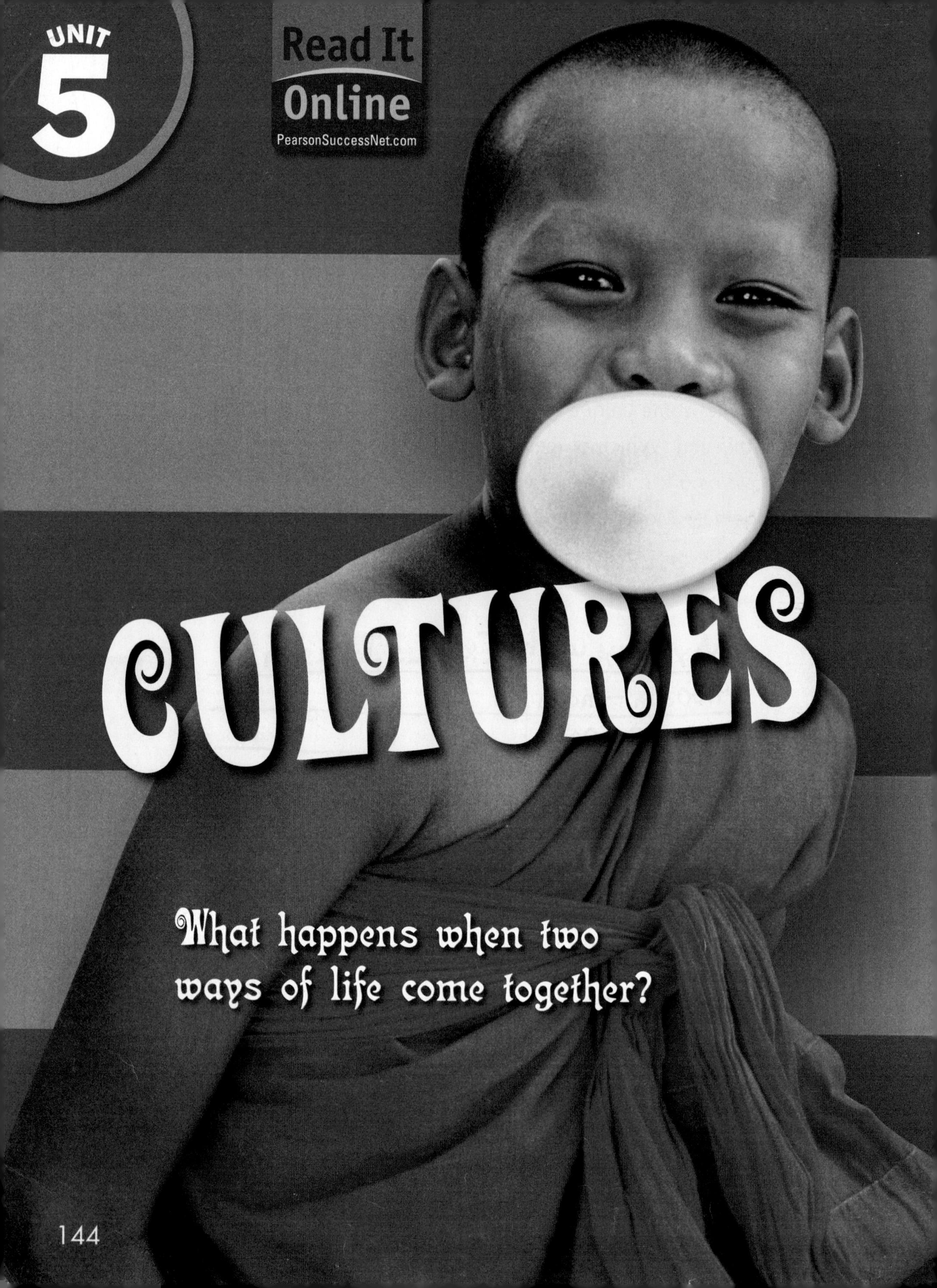

CULTURES

What happens when two ways of life come together?

Suki's Kimono

Suki doesn't care that
her outfit is unusual.

REALISTIC FICTION

connect to SOCIAL STUDIES

How My Family Lives in America

Three children with
different backgrounds
tell about their traditions.

NARRATIVE NONFICTION

connect to SOCIAL STUDIES

Good-Bye, 382 Shin Dang Dong

Jangmi makes a difficult
move to a new country.

REALISTIC FICTION

connect to SOCIAL STUDIES

Jalapeño Bagels

Pablo shares a special
food that is a mixture of
his parents' cultures.

REALISTIC FICTION

connect to SOCIAL STUDIES

Me and Uncle Romie

A boy from the country lives
in the city for a while.

REALISTIC FICTION

connect to SOCIAL STUDIES

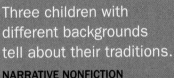

145

Comprehension

Skill
Compare
and Contrast

Strategy
Predict

Skill

Compare
and Contrast

- When you compare and contrast two or more things, you tell how they are alike and different.

- Some clue words that signal that things might be the same are *like, same, both, also,* and *as well as.*

- Some clue words that signal differences are *but, however, different,* and *instead of.*

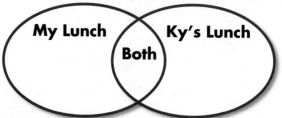

Strategy

Strategy: Predict

Active readers predict what might happen next based on what they have already read. Predicting helps readers think more about what they read. They can predict what might be the same or different.

Write to Read

1. Read "The Boxed Lunch." Create a diagram like the one above to compare what you eat for lunch to Ky's lunch.

2. Write a short paragraph comparing the two lunches.

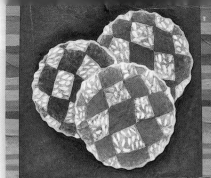

THE BOXED LUNCH

Ky was nervous about his first day in his new school. But he knew for sure he would like his lunch. It would be the same as his lunches in Japan, even though he now was in America.

In Japan, Ky always brought his lunch in a bento box, which was carefully packed with eye-catching foods. Ky loved the sausage that looked like a tiny octopus. Instead of carrot sticks, he had hard-boiled eggs that looked like baby chicks just hatching. And instead of tortilla chips, he had a rice ball covered with pieces of dried seaweed so that it looked like a soccer ball. ●————

Skill Here are some clue words—*instead of.* What is being compared? Are they the same or different?

At lunchtime, when Ky's classmates began eating their lunches, someone said, "Ky, what did you bring for lunch?" ●————

Strategy Here is a good place to stop and predict. What do you think Ky's new classmates will think of what he brought for lunch?

Ky opened his box slowly, not sure of what his new friends would think. But they were very interested. He explained each item and showed them how to eat with chopsticks. Some boys asked to try the chopsticks. Ky promised to bring some for everyone the next day. His new friends laughed. One friend said, "I wonder how they'll work with peanut butter and jelly sandwiches."

festival

snug

rhythm

paces

graceful

pale

cotton

handkerchief

Remember

Try the strategy. Then, if you need more help, use your glossary or a dictionary.

Vocabulary Strategy
for Synonyms

Context Clues Sometimes when you are reading, you might see a word you don't know. The author may have used a synonym that will give you a clue. A synonym is a word that has the same or almost the same meaning as another word. For example, *difficult* is a synonym for *hard.* Look for a word that might be a synonym. The word you know can help you understand the meaning of the word you don't know.

1. Look at the words and sentences near the unknown word. The author may have used a synonym.

2. Do you recognize a word that might be a synonym?

3. Try the synonym in place of the unknown word. Does it make sense?

Read "Pass It Down." Look for synonyms to help you understand the meanings of the vocabulary words.

Pass It Down

Emily Douglas is named after her grandmother, Emily Kelly. Every summer Emily Kelly's village in Ireland held a dance festival and contest. Emily K. was 8 the first time she entered the contest. She had practiced for weeks, but she was very nervous and started to worry. One shoe felt comfortably snug while the other felt too tight. When the fiddles began playing, her heart was thumping so loudly that she couldn't hear the rhythm. So she started a few paces, or steps, behind the beat. That's the way she did the entire dance! When she finished, everyone applauded and cheered. The judges told her how graceful she was and how original her dance was! She won first prize–a pale blue cotton handkerchief embroidered with white flowers. When Emily K. came to the United States, the handkerchief was one of the few things she brought with her. Later she gave it to her granddaughter Emily. The blue is even lighter now and the cotton is very thin. But Emily has kept the handkerchief. It makes her think about another young girl named Emily.

Words to Write

Do you know a story about someone in your family? Write it down or make one up. Use words from the Words to Know list if you can.

Suki's Kimono

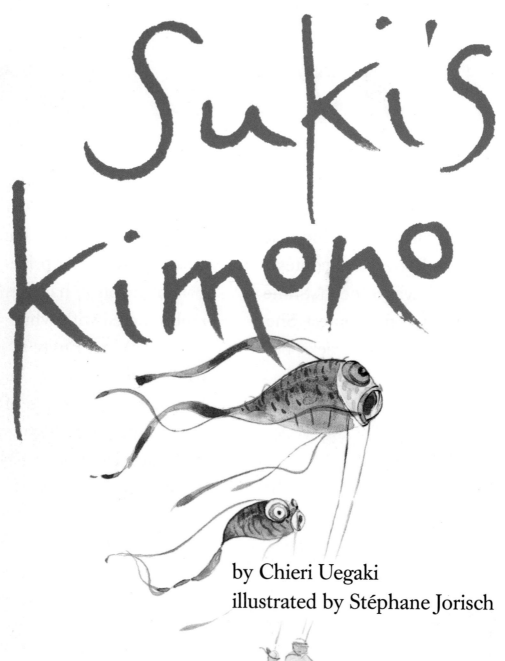

by Chieri Uegaki
illustrated by Stéphane Jorisch

Genre   **Realistic fiction** has characters and events that are like people and events in real life. Does Suki remind you of someone you know?

What is special about Suki's kimono?

On the first day of school, Suki wanted to wear her kimono. Her sisters did not approve.

"You can't wear that," said Mari. "People will think you're weird."

"You can't wear that," said Yumi. "Everyone will laugh, and no one will play with you."

"You need something new, Suki."

"You need something cool."

But Suki shook her head. She didn't care for new. She didn't care for cool. She wanted to wear her favorite thing. And her favorite thing was her kimono.

Suki's obāchan had given her the kimono. The first time Suki wore it, her obāchan took her to a street festival where they slurped bowls of slippery, cold sōmen noodles and shared a cone of crunchy, shaved ice topped with a sweet red bean sauce.

Under strings of paper lanterns, Suki joined her obāchan in a circle dance. She followed her and copied her movements, trying to be as light and as graceful. She watched the other women and children who danced, especially those who were dressed in cotton kimonos like her.

Later, Suki sat so close to the stage that when the taiko drummers performed, *bom-bom-bom-bom,* she felt like she'd swallowed a ball of thunder, and her whole insides quaked and quivered.

Before they left the festival, Suki and her obāchan stopped at a souvenir stand. There were many things to choose from, but her obāchan found the prettiest thing of all—a handkerchief of pale pink linen, decorated with tiny maple leaves and cherry blossoms. When she gave it to Suki, she said, "This will help you remember our day."

Now, it was time for school. Mother checked Suki's obi one last time and took a picture of Mari, Yumi, and Suki together by the front steps.

Then, as she watched, the three sisters made their way down the block to their school. Mari and Yumi stayed several paces ahead of Suki and pretended they didn't know her.

But Suki didn't mind.

She turned and waved to her mother before she clip-clopped along in her shiny red geta, feeling very pleased in her fan-patterned blue kimono.

Once in a while, Suki would lift her arms and let the butterfly sleeves flutter in the breeze. It made her feel like she'd grown her own set of wings.

When they reached the school, Mari and Yumi hurried across the yard to a group of their friends. Suki stopped and looked around. Some of the children turned and stared at her, and others giggled and pointed at her kimono.

But Suki ignored them.

She took a seat on a swing
to wait for the bell. A girl dressed
in overalls just like a pair Suki had
at home sat on the swing beside her.

"Hi, Suki," said the girl.

"Hi, Penny," said Suki.

"How come you're dressed so funny?" Penny asked.
"Where did you get those shoes?"

Suki lifted her feet off the sand and wiggled her
toes. "I'm not dressed funny," she said. "My grandma
gave me these shoes."

Suki started pumping her legs. After a moment,
Penny did the same, and soon they were both
swinging as fast and as high as they could. *Swoosh,
swoosh,* up and up.

When the bell rang, Suki and Penny jumped off their swings and ran to the gym for the first day assembly. Once they were finally taken to their new classroom, Suki chose a desk near the window. Penny chose a desk next to Suki.

As they waited for everyone to find a seat, two boys in front of Suki turned and snickered behind their hands. One of the boys reached over and snatched at Suki's sleeve. "Look at this," he said. "She's a bat!"

Suki felt her cheeks burn, but she did not respond. Instead, she concentrated on sitting up straight and tall, the way her obāchan always did. It was easy to do with an obi wrapped snug around her middle. Her obi was golden yellow, and in its folds Suki had tucked away her pale pink handkerchief.

"Welcome to the first grade," said the teacher. "My name is Mrs. Paggio." She smiled. "Let's introduce ourselves and tell everyone what we did this summer."

When it was her turn to speak, Suki stood up and told the teacher her name.

"Hello, Suki," said Mrs. Paggio. "What did you do this summer?"

"My grandma visited us," she said, straightening her sleeves. "She brought me my kimono and my geta." Suki raised her foot to show the teacher her wooden clog.

Somewhere in the classroom, someone laughed, but Suki took a deep breath and continued. "The best thing was that she took me to a festival. And there were dancing girls, dressed like me, and they danced like this." She took a few steps and swayed her arms sideways.

"Look, now she's *dancing*," someone said. But Suki didn't hear.

She hummed the music she remembered hearing at the festival.

She remembered how it felt to dance barefoot in the open air, on fresh-cut grass that tickled her toes.

She tried to picture the other dancers. How they moved forward in the circle with the rhythm of the music. How they stamped their feet, first right, then left, swung their arms, first up, then down. How they stepped back, and back, and back, then clapped.

When Suki couldn't remember the next step, she made it up, just to keep dancing. *One-two, one-two, one-two, stop.*

When she finished, the room seemed very quiet. Everyone was watching her.

Suki sat down, wondering if she was in trouble.

But Mrs. Paggio said, "That was wonderful, Suki."
And she started to clap.
Then, so did Penny.
And after a moment, so did the entire class.

After school, as the three sisters
walked home together, Mari and Yumi
grumbled about their first day.

"No one even noticed my new sweater,"
said Mari.

"No one even noticed my cool shoes,"
said Yumi.

But Suki just smiled.

As she clip-clopped along behind them, Suki pulled
out the pale pink handkerchief from her obi and held
it up over her head to catch the wind. And in her blue
cotton kimono and in her shiny red geta, Suki danced
all the way home.

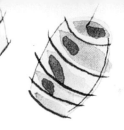

Reader Response

Open for Discussion Pretend that you are Suki. Suki, why didn't you wear something new and cool to school? Tell about your first day at school.

1. If you read carefully, you get to know Suki. How does the author help you do that? **Think Like an Author**

2. At school, Suki meets her friend Penny. How are Penny's clothes different from Suki's? **Compare and Contrast**

3. What prediction did you make when Suki began telling the class about her kimono? What helped you make your prediction? Was it correct? **Predict**

4. The words *paces* and *rhythm* and *graceful* might be used in a description of Suki's dance for her class. Write that description for a class newspaper using those and other words from the Words to Know list and from the story.
Vocabulary

Look Back and Write What two foods did Suki and her *obāchan* eat at the street festival? Look back at page 153. Then write and draw what they were.

Meet author **Chieri Uegaki on page 419.**

Write Now

Editorial

Prompt

Suki's Kimono tells about a girl who dresses the way she wants instead of like everyone else. Think about why it is important to be yourself. Now write an editorial about this issue.

Student Model

In the first sentence, the editorial <u>focuses</u> on the <u>main idea.</u> **All the details in the other sentences support the main idea.**

Being yourself should be the easiest thing to do, but sometimes it is hard for kids. At school, someone is always deciding what is and is not cool. For example, someone may say one kind of sneaker is the coolest. Then all the other kids beg their parents for those shoes. Maybe they cost a lot of money. Not everyone can afford them. Also, everyone has different ideas. Maybe you like a different kind of shoes better. Why should you get the "cool" kind just to fit in with the group? So start out right. Follow your own style now!

Writer urges readers to take a specific action in the final sentence.

Use the model to help you write your own editorial.

Clothes
Bringing Cultures Together

by Elizabeth Massie

Next time you walk through town, look at the clothes people are wearing. You might see ponchos, blue jeans, and sneakers. You might see moccasins (MOK-uh-sunz), t-shirts, and berets (bur-AYZ). Many of the clothes we wear today are new designs. However, some were first made in other countries or by other cultures long ago. They have become part of modern American fashion.

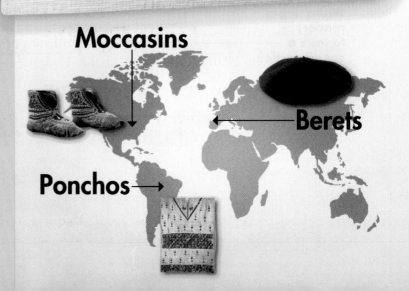

Moccasins

Berets

Ponchos

South American Ponchos

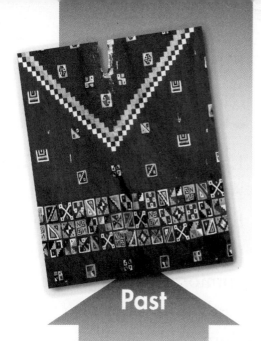

Thousands of years ago, people of South America made and wore ponchos. A poncho is a square cloak. It has a hole in the middle for the wearer's head.

South American ponchos were woven out of wool. The wool came from llamas and other pack animals. The ponchos were often decorated with flowers, birds, and people. Ponchos kept the wearers warm in cold weather.

Ponchos are still part of everyday wear in many South American countries. The style is much the same as it was long ago.

During the 20th century, people in the United States began to wear ponchos. Americans liked their style and warmth. Ponchos were also adapted into rain gear. Rain ponchos are made of waterproof material. They often have hoods.

Past

The poncho above was made in South America more than two thousand years ago. You might see the ponchos below on our streets today.

Present

 Predict What do you think you will learn about?

167

Native American Moccasins

Long ago, native people of North America made shoes out of animal hides. These shoes were called moccasins. Moccasins were tough and comfortable. They kept the wearer's feet warm. They also protected feet from cold, rough ground.

Moccasin styles were different from tribe to tribe. You could tell what tribe people belonged to by looking at their shoes. For example, the Blackfeet tribe was called that because they dyed their moccasins black.

Native Americans taught European settlers how to make moccasins. Trappers and explorers wore these shoes in the wilderness. Even Lewis and Clark made and wore moccasins on their trip west.

Today, Americans of many backgrounds wear moccasins. They like the soft comfort of the shoe.

Past

Members of the Blackfeet tribe (top) wore moccasins that were dyed black. These colorful moccasins (above) were made years ago by Native Americans. The moccasins below are similar to those worn today.

Present

Compare and Contrast How are moccasins like the shoes you are wearing?

Basque
Berets

A beret is a soft, round hat. Hundreds of years ago, the Basque (BASK) people made these hats out of wool. Basque shepherds tended their flocks in the cold mountains between France and Spain. These hats kept their heads warm.

In the 1920s, British tank soldiers started wearing black berets. The hats were comfortable. They didn't show grease stains. During World War II, some British soldiers gave American soldiers berets to wear. The hats were seen as special. Today, some units of the United States military wear berets.

Berets became popular with American women in the 1930s. Berets are still worn by men, women, and children as part of everyday outfits.

Past

British General Bernard Law Montgomery, above, popularized the use of berets during World War II. Even today, traditional clothes for Basque men, below, often include berets.

Present

Reading Across Texts
The author of "Clothes: Bringing Cultures Together" describes ponchos, moccasins, and berets. How might she describe Suki's kimono?
Writing Across Texts Write your description.

Fact and Opinion

- A statement of fact can be proved true or false.

- A statement of opinion gives someone's thoughts or feelings about something. Words that express feelings, such as *favorite* and *wonderful,* are clues that this might be an opinion.

Facts	Opinions

Strategy: Text Structure

Good readers notice when authors organize their writing to compare and contrast. Some clue words that signal a compare and contrast structure are *however, on the other hand, but,* and *although.* Writing that compares often includes facts and opinions. As a reader, you must watch for these.

Write to Read

1. Read "The Best Game." Make a chart like the one above. Fill it in as you read.

2. Write a short paragraph about your favorite game using facts and opinions.

The Best Game

I think board games are the best family activity. Playing a board game with family or friends is my favorite thing to do on a rainy day. However, my sister doesn't agree. She likes playing charades with a group. To her, board games are boring.

Skill This paragraph includes some opinions. What are they? What clue words do you see?

Board games include everything you need right in the box. There is nothing to think up or to make. The rules are printed out. That's the best part! There shouldn't be any arguments among players. Hundreds of board games are sold every year. The people who buy them can't all be wrong.

On the other hand, my sister favors charades. She says it's a creative game. Players must think of books, movies, or songs that will stump the other team. Players use their imagination and always have a great time.

Strategy Here is a clue that signals a compare and contrast text structure. What is it?

Here you have two kinds of games, two people, and two ideas. Which game is best? You decide.

How My Family Lives in America

Words to Know

famous

overnight

mention

twist

admire

popular

custom

public

Remember

Try the strategy. Then, if you need more help, use your glossary or a dictionary.

Vocabulary Strategy
for Antonyms

Context Clues Sometimes when you are reading, you come across a word you don't know. The author might use an antonym for the word that will give you a clue. An antonym is a word that means the opposite of another word. For example, *huge* is the opposite of *tiny*. Look for another word that might be an antonym. It can help you understand the meaning of the word you don't know.

1. Look at the words and sentence around the unknown word. The author may have used an antonym.

2. Look for words that seem to have opposite meanings. Think about the one word you know.

3. Use that word to help you figure out the meaning of its antonym.

Read "A Rising Star." Look for antonyms to help you understand the meanings of the vocabulary words.

A Rising Star

Enrique Garza is a famous film star now. But not so long ago he was just an unknown actor from Puerto Rico. Many people think that happened overnight.

Mention this to Enrique and he laughs. He acted in movies and television for ten years in Puerto Rico. Then he came to the United States. After five years and a few small parts, he got his big break in *The Big Twist*. Since then he has been in eight movies.

Some critics admire his work. Others criticize the movies he has chosen to do. Enrique says he does not care whether his movies are popular or flops. He only wants to do the best job he can.

Reporters know they should not ask him about his family. It is his custom to answer such questions with comments about the weather! He says he wants to keep his private life and his public life separate. He will tell you that he goes back to Puerto Rico as often as he can and that he always carries a small Puerto Rican flag with him to remind him of where he came from.

Words to Write

Write about a famous person whom you admire. Explain why you admire that person. Use words from the Words to Know list.

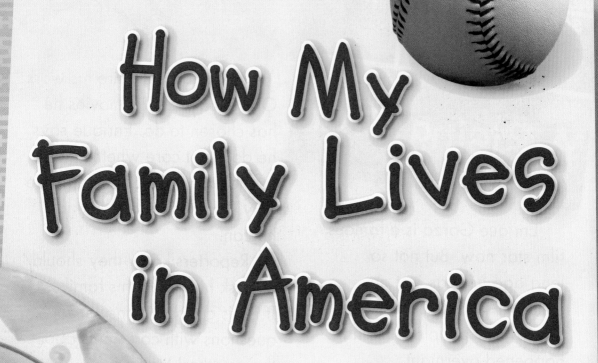

How My Family Lives in America

by Susan Kuklin

174

U.S.A.

How did these families bring their heritage to America?

Sanu, Eric, and April are American children with families just like yours. They have parents, grandparents, aunts, and uncles who love them and take care of them. Year after year, their families celebrate special days together in special ways. Because Sanu, Eric, and April each have at least one parent who did not grow up in the United States, their family heritage is an interesting mixture. Some traditions, remembered from a parent's childhood in another place, are kept alive in America. And sometimes, with the help of Sanu, Eric, and April, new traditions are started.

Here are their stories.

My name is Sanu. A long time ago, Sanu was a princess in Africa. My brother, Badu, was named after a famous warrior. He's glad about that.

We have these names because my daddy was born in Senegal, a country far away in West Africa. He moved to America to go to college. My *maam bou djigen* and *maam bou gor*, which means "daddy's mommy" and "daddy's daddy" in a language people speak in Senegal, still live there. When we visited them last year, I learned all about the Senegalese part of me. I learned to call Mommy *Yay* and Daddy *Bay*. Maam bou djigen and Maam bou gor gave Badu a drum and African clothing. He dresses African style every chance he gets.

AFRICA

Senegal

maam bou djigen (mahm boo deejen)

maam bou gor (mahm boo gore)

Yay (yah´ ee)

Bay (bah´ ee)

That's me.

177

I have an American grandmother too. She lives in a city called Baltimore, where my mother grew up. My mommy's mommy comes to visit us in New York City on weekends. Then she teaches me about good manners, about being neat and clean, about standing straight and tall.

Grandma sings to us the songs she taught Mommy. Our favorites are "Precious Lord Take My Hand" and "Hush Little Baby Don't You Cry." When Badu tries to play along on his African drum, it doesn't sound like Africa.

During the week, I go to Mommy's work after school to help out. The thing I like about my mommy's hairdressing shop is that it reminds me of how people look in Senegal. In my daddy's village, the girls weave a kind of cloth into their braid. This is called a Senegalese twist. I'm only five, so I'm still learning how to make a regular braid.

This is an eggplant.

Sometimes Daddy picks me up after his work and takes me shopping for food. Daddy knows how to cook African style. Together we buy carrots, cabbage, eggplant, tomatoes, yams, and cassava, a vegetable that is like a potato.

Daddy likes to tease Mommy. "In Africa the wife gets the food and cooks it too."

"You're in America now," my mommy says, laughing.

For a special meal my daddy fixes *tiebou dienn* for lunch, just like his family has in Senegal. Tiebou dienn is rice and fish and vegetables. For this meal, we invite my daddy's relatives, Fifi, Sambo, and Hussane, to join us.

tiebou dienn (chéb-oo-jenn)

179

Before we eat, we all wash our hands the way we did in my father's village. I want everyone to hurry up.

"In Africa," my father says, "the children must be patient and wait their turn."

"You're in America now," I giggle.

At this meal, everyone dresses like people do in Senegal. We put a cloth on the floor, not on the table, since it is the custom to eat on the ground in Senegal. Everyone eats together from one big bowl. Here's the best part: we get to eat with our hands, not with forks and spoons.

Daddy shows us how to squeeze the oil out of the tiebou dienn. While we eat, we hear stories about our parents when they were little in Senegal and in Baltimore. Mommy says how lucky we are to be African Americans.

Yummy!

UNITED STATES

MEXICO

Puerto Rico

My name is Eric. I live in a tall apartment building in New York City with my mommy and daddy and our pet parrot called Pepí.

My daddy and all my grandparents came to New York from Puerto Rico. Daddy showed me how to find Puerto Rico on a map. It is an island in the ocean not too far from Florida. Mommy, Pepí, and I were born in New York City.

When Daddy comes home from work we play our favorite sport, baseball. It's hard to catch the ball when I wear my heavy winter jacket. Last winter Mommy and Daddy took me to Puerto Rico for a vacation. I learned lots of things about my heritage.

That's me.

Daddy grew up where there are palm trees, like in Florida. And it is warm every day in Puerto Rico, so warm that people can always play baseball without a jacket. Everyone in Puerto Rico speaks Spanish, just like my grandparents.

In our home we speak two languages, English and Spanish. Even Pepí speaks English and Spanish. My friends, Irma and Glen, speak Spanish too. They come from another island called the Dominican Republic. If you come from a place where people speak Spanish, you are called a *Hispanic.* We call ourselves Hispanic Americans because part of us is Spanish and part of us is American. In my city, there are lots of Hispanics from many different countries, but they all speak the same language, Spanish.

I'm throwing a pitch!

Sometimes Irma and Glen stop by to help me with my chores. We clean beans, then set them in a pot of water overnight to make them soft. Then Mommy shows me how to crush garlic for *sofrito*, which is a mixture of Spanish spices that will go into the bean pot.

The next night, Mommy, Daddy, and I have our favorite dinner, *arroz con pollo y habichuelas*. It's rice with chicken and beans. Mommy and I are good cooks.

sofrito (so-frée-to)
arroz con pollo y habichuelas (a-rós kom bóy-jo ee a-bich-wél-as)

When my parents are at work, my mommy's mommy, Nana Carmen, takes me shopping at the *carniceria,* the Spanish meat market. I get to pay.

"*Muchas gracias,*" the grocer says to thank me. To answer, I say, "*De nada,*" which means "don't mention it."

My nana Carmen visits me every single day. At bedtime she comes to our home just to kiss me good night. Sometimes she shows me her tiny hurts so I can tell her my special Spanish healing poem:

Sana, sana, sana.
Si no te curas hoy,
Te curas mañana.

Heal, heal, heal.
If you don't heal today,
You'll heal tomorrow.

carniceria (kar nees-eriá)

Muchas gracias
(móo-chas gráss-ee-as)

De nada (day natha)

Nana's tiny hurt

When Mommy is home from work, she plays Spanish music on the stereo. Then my friends, Mommy, and I dance the *merengue*. When we hear the music, we shake our hips and move to the beat: one-two, one-two. In Spanish we count like this: *uno, dos*.

In my family, next to baseball, we love Spanish dances best. When my *madrina*, that's my godmother, stops in for a visit, she dances with us. Sometimes Daddy, Nana Carmen, and my friends' mommy join in.

And Pepí sings, "¡MERENGUE!"

merengue (me-rén-gay)

uno (oono)

dos (dose)

madrina (ma-drée-na)

¡MERENGUE!

185

My name in America is April. I also have a Chinese name: *Chin,* which means "admire" and *Lan,* which means "orchid."

Both my parents are Chinese and were born in Taiwan. Taiwan is an island on the other side of the world. My papa came to New York without his parents to go to school, and my mama moved here with her family. Because Julius, my older brother, and May, my older sister, and I were born in America, we are called Chinese Americans.

There are many Chinese Americans. But we do not all speak the same Chinese language. The way my family speaks Chinese is called *Mandarin.*

In Mandarin, I call my daddy *baba* and my mommy *mama.* It sounds something like English, but when we write the words they look very different. Another thing that's different in Chinese is that words aren't made with letters. Each word has its own special marks.

爸
爸
father

媽
媽
mother

Here I am.

Chin Lan (ching lan)
baba (bah-bah)
mama (mah-mah)

My teacher helps me.

During the week we go to public school, but on Saturday we go to Chinese school. There we learn how to speak and write in Chinese, like my parents learned in Taiwan. When I write English letters, I write from the left side of the page to the right. When I write in Chinese, I write from the right to the left. And I write in rows from the top of the page to the bottom. For us Chinese American kids, there are many things to remember.

In Chinese school we also learn a special kind of writing called *calligraphy.* We use a brush instead of a pen, black ink, and special paper made from stalks of rice. Our teacher shows us the right way to hold the brush.

芝蔴涼麵

cold
sesame
noodles

八

eight

My favorite part of Chinese school is snack time. Today, Mama made me cold sesame noodles, *tsu ma liang mein.* I eat them with a fork, but most Chinese people eat their noodles with chopsticks. I'm just learning to eat with chopsticks.

Papa told us that an Italian explorer named Marco Polo discovered noodles in China a long time ago and introduced them to his country.

When Mama brought home takeout, Julius asked if a Chinese explorer discovered pizza in Italy.

Mama and Papa laughed and said, "No."

While we eat our pizza we play a game to test our wits. Papa asks us to look for letters hidden in the picture on the pizza box. Julius sees a *V* in the pizza man's shoe. May finds an *L*.

Oh, look! I can even see the Chinese letter *Ba*, in the pizza man's eyebrows. *Ba* means "eight" in Chinese.

tsu ma liang mein (tsu mah leeang mee-en)
Ba (bah)

At night when we have finished all our chores and all our homework, we play *Chi chiao bang*. In America some people call it *Tangram*. This is a popular game in Taiwan, like checkers is in America. My grandparents and even my great-grandparents played this game. To play, you move seven different shapes to build a new shape. I like to make a pussycat. It is very difficult, but I can do it. Papa says, "Go slowly and think about a cat. After a while your mind will start to run, and you will see the cat in the shapes." He's right.

There is an old Chinese saying, "The older you are, the wiser you become." When I become a grown-up, I will remember to tell this to my family.

七
巧
板

Chi
chiao
bang

Chi chiao bang
(chee chow bang)

I'm making a cat.

Reader Response

Open for Discussion Suppose that you visit Sanu, Eric, and April all in one day. Tell the three best things that happen during each visit.

1. How does the author show you that these are real children? Choose three parts of the selection to help you explain. **Think Like an Author**

2. The selection is full of facts. Find some. How could you prove that these facts are true? **Fact and Opinion**

3. Each child in this selection compares America or American traditions with his or her native country or traditions. What clue words did you notice that helped you recognize a text structure? How did that help you as you read? **Text Structure**

4. Which of the three cultures you read about was most interesting to you? Tell why. Use words from the Words to Know list and from the story. **Vocabulary**

Look Back and Write Here is a riddle: Why is it easier to play baseball in winter in Puerto Rico than in New York? Look back at pages 181–182. Use information from the selection in your answer.

**Meet author and photographer
Susan Kuklin on page 420.**

Write Now

Write Your Opinion

Prompt

How My Family Lives in America describes traditions such as special foods.

Think of a kind of food that you have strong feelings about.

Now write an opinion about that kind of food, using persuasive words.

Student Model

Writer states opinion using a strong persuasive word.

Vivid details help make opinion more convincing.

Writer uses a variety of sentences— a question, a command, a statement, and an exclamation.

My parents moved to the United States from Mexico many years ago. Maybe that is why I love Mexican food. Mexican food is the best food in the world! Do you like spicy dishes? Try spicy tomato salsa made with hot peppers. Do you like green vegetables? Try a Mexican salad served in a crunchy tortilla. A taco filled with beef or chicken is great. Best of all, there are hundreds of different kinds of Mexican dishes! There is something delicious for everyone. It's the tastiest food you can eat!

Use the model to help you write your own opinion.

Textbook

Genre

- Textbooks provide information about a specific subject.
- Textbook passages include many facts.

Text Features

- The title tells the main idea of a section or chapter.
- In this selection, a summary of the lesson reviews the main points from the text.

Link to Social Studies

Use the library to research Cinco de Mayo and St. Patrick's Day. Make a poster advertising a community celebration for one of these holidays.

Communities Celebrate Cultures

Many communities have celebrations that started in other countries. The celebrations honor the ethnic groups who helped build the community. These celebrations are sometimes called ethnic celebrations.

Cinco de Mayo (SIN ko day MY oh) means the fifth of May. It is a Mexican holiday that celebrates the victory of the Mexican people over the French who invaded their country. After a battle on May 5, 1862, the French left Mexico.

Fact and Opinion Is this text mostly facts or opinions?

For many people, the holiday is a symbol. It shows that the people of Mexico could become free of rulers from other countries.

Today, many people in Mexico and other countries celebrate Cinco de Mayo. In the United States people dance in colorful clothes. They play music on guitars and eat traditional Mexican food. They show that they are proud to be Mexican Americans.

St. Patrick's Day is celebrated in many communities around the United States and the world. The holiday started as a religious holiday in Ireland, a country in Europe.

On St. Patrick's Day both Irish and non-Irish people celebrate Irish culture. Some people honor Irish culture by wearing green clothing, watching parades, and eating food that is dyed green.

REVIEW In what ways are Cinco de Mayo and St. Patrick's Day alike? How are they different?

Summarize the Lesson

- People follow traditions when they celebrate holidays.
- Families celebrate religious and non-religious holidays.
- Communities celebrate to honor ethnic groups who helped build their community.

Reading Across Texts

The children in *How My Family Lives in America* tell about cultural traditions different from those mentioned in this textbook article. Why do you think this is so?

Writing Across Texts Make a list of the many celebrations and traditions you learned about.

Comprehension

Skill
Sequence

Strategy
Monitor
and Fix Up

 # Sequence

- The sequence of a story is the order in which events happen.

- Clue words, such as *first*, *next*, *then*, and *finally*, are often used to signal the sequence of events. Dates and times can also be clues. Sometimes, no clue words are used at all.

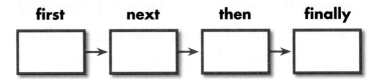

first	next	then	finally

 ## Strategy: Monitor and Fix Up

When something you read is confusing, one way to better understand is to read on. If you are confused by the order of events, keep reading to see if the events become clearer.

Write to Read

1. Read "Moving Day." Make a graphic organizer like the one above. Write the events of the story in sequence.

2. Write a short paragraph that summarizes the story in the correct order.

MOVING DAY

Tom's family was getting ready to move to Chicago. Tom's mom was starting a new job in two weeks. There was lots to do to get ready for moving day!

Mom and Dad decided to pack things that they didn't need every day. Tom would help. First, he helped his dad pack tools in the garage. After that, Tom helped his mom carefully wrap special treasures from the attic. When they were done, the house seemed strange and there were boxes everywhere.

> **Skill** Here are some clue words. In what order have events happened so far?

The day before moving day, Tom got up early to pack his own clothes. After lunch, Tom packed all of his toys and other belongings. When Tom went to bed that night, his room was almost empty.

> **Strategy** If you're confused here, read on. Events may become clearer.

Moving day finally arrived. While the movers loaded all of their belongings into the truck, Tom helped his parents make sure nothing was forgotten. It had been a tremendous amount of work to get ready for moving day!

Words to Know

homesick
airport
raindrops
memories
farewell
curious
described
delicious

Remember

Try the strategy. Then, if you need more help, use your glossary or a dictionary.

Vocabulary Strategy
for Compound Words

Word Structure Sometimes you may come across a long word when you are reading. Look closely at the word. Do you see two smaller words in it? It might be a compound word. You may be able to use the two small words to help you figure out the meaning of the compound word. For example, a *classroom* is a room where a class is held.

1. Divide the compound word into its two small words.

2. Think of the meaning of each small word. Put the two meanings together. Does this help you understand the meaning of the compound word?

3. Try the meaning in the sentence. Does it make sense?

Read "How to Do a Move." Use the meanings of the smaller words to help you understand the meanings of the compound words.

How to Do a Move

So you're moving. When you heard the news, did your stomach start to ache? Did you become homesick before you had even left? Don't wait until you get to the airport to get ready for a move. Start planning now.

- Recognize that, just as surely as raindrops are wet, you are going to be upset and unhappy. But that's OK. Just set a time limit. When the time is up, do something to make yourself feel better.
- Keep the memories. Take pictures of your old home, neighborhood, and friends. Make a scrapbook.
- Have a farewell party. Exchange addresses and telephone numbers with your friends.
- Be curious about your new town. Research the area at the library and on the Internet. It might be described in guidebooks. It might be known for a famous person or a delicious food. The more you know about the place, the more familiar it will feel when you get there.

Words to Write

Write about a move that you have made or what you think it would be like to move to a new place. Use words from the Words to Know list.

Good-Bye, 382 Shin Dang Dong

382 Shin Dang Dong

by Frances Park and Ginger Park

illustrated by Yangsook Choi

Genre

Realistic fiction tells about events that could happen in real life. Does anything in this selection remind you of an event from your life?

What is 382 Shin Dang Dong?

My heart beats in two places: Here, where I live, and also in a place where I once lived. You see, I was born in Korea. One day my parents told me we were moving to America. I was eight years old, old enough to keep many lovely memories of my birthplace alive in my heart forever. But one very sad memory stays with me too. The day I cried, "Good-bye, 382 Shin Dang Dong!"

On that summer day I woke up to the sound of light rain tapping on my window. The monsoon season was coming. I didn't even need to open my eyes to know that. It was that time of year. It was also time to move.

In a few hours, I would be on an airplane.

When I opened my eyes, my heart sank. My bedroom was so bare! No hand-painted scrolls or colorful fans on my walls. No silk cushions or straw mats on my floor. All my possessions were packed away in a big brown box marked "Lovely Things."

I frowned and listened to the raindrops. One, two, three . . . Soon the thick of the monsoon would arrive, and a thousand raindrops would hit our clay-tiled roof all at once. But I wouldn't be here to listen to them. I would be halfway around the world in a strange, foreign place called 112 Foster Terrace, Brighton, Massachusetts, U.S.A.

My parents were very excited.

"Jangmi, you will like America," Dad tried to assure me.

"Are the seasons the same?" I wondered.

"Oh, yes."

"With monsoon rains?"

"No, Jangmi, no monsoon rains."

"No friends either," I moaned.

"You will make many new friends in America," Mom promised me, "in your new home."

But I loved my home right here! I didn't want to go to America and make new friends. I didn't want to leave my best friend, Kisuni.

After breakfast, Kisuni and I ran out into the rain and to the open market. Monsoon season was also the season for sweet, yellow melons called *chummy.* Kisuni and I would often peel and eat chummy under the willow tree that stood outside my bedroom window. But today, the chummy were for guests who were coming over for a farewell lunch.

At the market we peered into endless baskets and took our time choosing the ripest, plumpest chummy we could find.

"Do they have chummy in America?" Kisuni wondered.

"No," I replied. "But my mom says they have melons called *honeydew.*"

"Honeydew," Kisuni giggled. "What a funny name!"

Soon after we returned, family and friends began to arrive, carrying pots and plates of food. One by one they took off their shoes, then entered the house. Grandmother was dressed in her most special occasion *hanbok*. She set up the long *bap sang* and before I could even blink, on it were a big pot of dumpling soup and the prettiest pastel rice cakes I had ever seen. Kisuni and I peeled and sliced our chummy and carefully arranged the pieces on a plate.

Then everybody ate and sang traditional Korean songs and celebrated in a sad way. Love and laughter and tears rippled through our house. How I wanted to pack these moments into a big brown box and bring them with me to America.

Kisuni and I sneaked outside and sat beneath the willow tree. We watched the rain with glum faces.

"Kisuni, I wish we never had to move from this spot," I said.

"Me, too," she sighed. "Jangmi, how far away is America?"

"My mom says that it's halfway around the world. And my dad told me that when the moon is shining here, the sun is shining there. That's how far apart we'll be," I moaned.

"That's really far," Kisuni moaned back.

We watched the rain and grew more glum than ever. Then Kisuni perked up.

"So when you're awake, I'll be asleep. And when I'm awake, you'll be asleep," she declared. "At least we'll always know what the other one is doing."

That moment our faces brightened. But a moment later we had to say good-bye.

Kisuni held back her tears. "Promise you'll write to me, Jangmi."

"I promise, Kisuni."

It was time to go to the airport.

"Kimpo Airport," Dad instructed the taxi driver.

The taxi slowly pulled away. I looked at our beautiful home one last time. Like rain on the window, tears streaked down my face.

"Good-bye, 382 Shin Dang Dong!" I cried.

On the long ride to the airport, Dad asked me, "Do you want to know what your new home looks like?"

"Okay," I shrugged.

"Let's see," Dad began, "it's a row house."

"A house that's attached to other houses," Mom explained.

"And inside the house are wooden floors," Dad added.

"No *ondal* floors?" I asked him. "How will we keep warm in the winter without ondal floors?"

"There are radiators in every room!" Mom said with an enthusiastic clap. "And a fireplace in the living room! Imagine!"

No, I could not imagine that. In our home we had a fire in the cellar called the *ondal.* It stayed lit all the time. The heat from the ondal traveled through underground pipes and kept our wax-covered floors warm and cozy. A fireplace in the living room sounded peculiar to me.

"And the rooms are separated by wooden doors," Mom added.

"No rice-paper doors?" I wondered.

My parents shook their heads.

"No, Jangmi."

My eyes closed with disappointment. I had a hard time picturing this house. Would it ever feel like home?

On the airplane, I sat by the window. We flew over rice fields and clay-tiled roofs. Already I felt homesick.

The next thing I knew, we were flying over the ocean. At first I could see fishing boats rocking in the waters. As we climbed higher into the clouds, the boats grew smaller and smaller. Suddenly, the world looked very big to me.

"Good-bye, 382 Shin Dang Dong," I cried again.

Dad sat back in his seat and began to read an American newspaper. The words were all foreign.

"Dad," I asked, "how will I ever learn to understand English?"

"It's not so hard," he said. "Would you like to learn an English word?"

"Okay," I sighed.

After a pause, Dad came up with—

"Rose."

"Rose?" I repeated. "What does that mean?"

"That's the English translation of your Korean name," Mom said.

"Rose means Jangmi?" I asked.

"Yes," my parents nodded.

"Rose," I said over and over.

"Would you like to adopt Rose as your American name?" Mom asked me.

"No, I like *my* name," I insisted.

On a foggy morning four days later, we arrived in Massachusetts. After we gathered our luggage, we climbed into an airport taxi.

Even through the fog, I could see that things were very different in America. There were big, wide roads called *highways*. The rooftops were shingled instead of clay-tiled. People shopped in glass-enclosed stores instead of open markets. No rice fields, no monsoon rains. So many foreign faces.

Slowly, the taxi pulled up to a row house on a quiet street. Red brick steps led up to a wooden door.

"Here we are, Jangmi," Dad said, "112 Foster Terrace, Brighton, Massachusetts, U.S.A."

The house was just as my parents had described. I took off my shoes and walked on wooden floors. They felt very cold. I opened wooden doors. They felt very heavy. Outside, the fog had lifted. But inside, everything felt dark and strange.

"Look," Dad pointed out the window, "there's a tree just like the one at home."

"No, it's not, Dad. It's not a willow tree," I said.

"No," he agreed. "It's a maple tree. But isn't it beautiful?"

382 Shin Dang Dong, 382 Shin Dang Dong. I wanted to go home to 382 Shin Dang Dong right now. Only a knock at the door saved me from tears.

Mom announced, "The movers are here!"

The house quickly filled up with furniture and big brown boxes. The box marked "Lovely Things" was the last to arrive.

I unpacked all my possessions. I hung my hand-painted scrolls and colorful fans on the walls. I placed my silk cushions and straw mats on the floor.

Then came another knock. To our surprise a parade of neighbors waltzed in carrying plates of curious food. There were pink-and-white iced cakes and warm pans containing something called *casseroles*.

A girl my age wandered up to me with a small glass bowl. Inside the bowl were colorful balls. They smelled fruity.

She pointed to a red ball and said, "Watermelon!" She pointed to an orange ball and said, "Cantaloupe!" Lastly she pointed to a green ball and said, "Honeydew!"

I took a green ball and tasted it. Mmm . . . it was as sweet and delicious as chummy.

The girl asked me a question. But I couldn't understand her.

"She wants to know what kind of fruit you eat in Korea," Dad stepped in.

"Chummy," I replied.

"Chummy," the girl repeated, then giggled—just like Kisuni!

She asked me another question.

"She wants to know your name," Dad said.

Maybe someday I would adopt Rose as my American name. But not today.

"Jangmi," I replied.

"Jangmi," the girl smiled. "My name is Mary."

"Mary," I smiled back.

I had made a new friend.

Later, when all the guests had gone, I went outside and sat under the maple tree. Dad was right, it *was* beautiful. Maybe someday Mary and I would sit beneath this tree and watch the rain fall. And maybe I would come to love it as much as our willow tree back home in Korea. But not today.

I began to write.

Dear Kisuni . . .

My best friend was so far away from me. So very, very far. But at least I knew where Kisuni was and what she was doing. She was halfway around the world, sleeping to the sound of a thousand raindrops hitting her clay-tiled roof all at once.

Reader Response

Open for Discussion If you moved to another land, what would you miss? What would you take with you? How would your move be like Jangmi's move?

1. Why do you think the authors wrote this story? Look at Meet the Authors on page 418 for ideas.
Think Like an Author

2. Make a time line showing the sequence of events during Jangmi's first day in her new home. Sequence

3. Was anything in this story confusing at first? How did you figure out the parts that were unclear? Did reading on help you? Monitor and Fix Up

4. Write an e-mail message that Jangmi might send Kisuni. In it, tell some things Americans have instead of chummy, ondal floors, and rice paper doors. Use words from the Words to Know list and from the story. Vocabulary

Look Back and Write In what did Jangmi pack her things to take to America? How did she feel about that? Look back at page 200. Use details from the story in your answer.

Meet authors **Frances and Ginger Park on page 418.**

216

Write Now

Ad

Prompt

In *Good-Bye, 382 Shin Dang Dong*, the narrator describes the market in Korea where she buys melons.

Think about a market, store, or shop that sells interesting items.

Now write an ad for this place, using vivid words.

Writing Trait

Vivid **word choice** makes a store or a product appeal to a reader. Use words that appeal to the senses.

Student Model

Inviting image in first sentence grabs readers' attention.

Come get your plump blueberries, juicy strawberries, and sweet peaches! In the summer, you should shop at Bob's Farm Stand. You'll find every fruit you can think of. Plus, Bob sells ripe tomatoes, crisp green beans, and crunchy lettuce.

Vivid <u>word choice</u> appeals to readers' senses.

Best of all, these delicious foods were just picked from nearby fields. So the next time you have a cookout, serve a fat watermelon or golden corn on the cob from Bob's. This summer, shop at Bob's for all your fruits and vegetables!

Ad makes direct appeal in last sentence.

Use the model to help you write your own ad.

217

Poetry

It's a Small World

words and music by Richard M. Sherman
and Robert B. Sherman

Song

Genre

- A song is a poem that is set to music. You can read the words of a song as you would a poem.

- In a song, often a refrain, or chorus, is repeated after every verse.

- Each verse of a song is similar to a stanza of a poem.

Link to Writing

Work with a small group to write another verse for the song. Add all the new verses to the original song, and try singing it as a class.

Verse

1. It's a world of laughter,
a world of tears,
It's a world of hopes
and a world of fears.
There's so much that we share,
and it's time we're aware,
It's a small world after all.

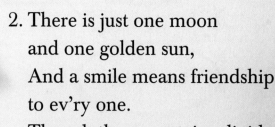

2. There is just one moon
and one golden sun,
And a smile means friendship
to ev'ry one.
Though the mountains divide
and the oceans are wide,
It's a small world after all.

Refrain

It's a small world after all,
It's a small world after all,
It's a small world after all,
It's a small, small world.

Reading Across Texts

Do you think Jangmi would agree with the first two lines of the song "It's a Small World"?

Writing Across Texts

Write a brief paragraph telling why you think as you do.

Monitor and Fix Up   Reread the song if you didn't understand the meaning.

Skill
Draw Conclusions

Strategy
Summarize

 # Draw Conclusions

- A conclusion is a decision or opinion that makes sense based on facts and details.

- You can also use what you already know to draw a conclusion.

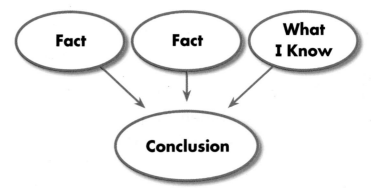

Fact

Fact

What I Know

Conclusion

 ## Strategy: Summarize

Good readers stop often and sum up what they've read so far. This helps them understand what they have read and provides background for drawing conclusions. A summary lists the important ideas without the details.

Write to Read

1. Read "What Does a Baker Do?" and make a graphic organizer like the one above.

2. Use the graphic organizer to write a paragraph that tells some of the things a baker does. Use your conclusion as the topic sentence for your paragraph.

What Does a Baker Do?

Have you ever helped an adult bake something? A baker is a person who makes baked goods for a living. A baker makes bread, cakes, pies, and many other tasty treats!

Skill Here is a good place to stop and draw a conclusion. What conclusion can you draw about bakers?

Some bakers work in large stores, some work in small neighborhood bakeries, and some work in restaurants. Baked goods must be fresh, so bakers often get up early in the morning to make goods to be sold the same day.

Bakers need to know what kinds of treats people in their neighborhood like. This helps them know what to make and how much to make.

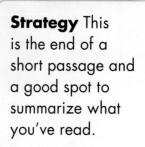

Many bakers learn their job by working with experienced bakers. They watch, listen, and practice on the job. Some bakers go to special schools to learn how to bake.

Bakers must know how to follow a recipe. Some bakers like to experiment and create their own recipes for their customers' favorite baked goods. Working as a baker can be an exciting career!

Strategy This is the end of a short passage and a good spot to summarize what you've read.

221

bakery

ingredients

batch

mixture

dough

knead

braided

boils

Remember

Try the strategy. Then, if you need more help, use your glossary or a dictionary.

Vocabulary Strategy
for Unfamiliar Words

Context Clues Sometimes when you are reading, you come across a word you don't know. How can you figure out what the word means? Look at the context, or the words and sentences around the word. You might find clues that can help you figure out the meaning of the word.

1. Read the words and sentences around the word you don't know. Sometimes the author tells you what the word means.

2. If not, use the words and sentences to predict a meaning for the word.

3. Try that meaning in the sentence. Does it make sense?

Read "Biscuits for Breakfast." Use context clues to help you understand the meanings of the vocabulary words.

Biscuits for Breakfast

Would you like something for breakfast that you will not find in a bakery? Make biscuits! You'll need only a few ingredients to make one batch.

1/3 cup shortening
1 3/4 cups flour
2 1/2 teaspoons baking powder
3/4 teaspoon salt
3/4 cup milk

Use a fork to add the shortening to the flour, baking powder, and salt. The mixture should look like fine crumbs. Add enough milk so that the dough rounds into a ball. Put the dough on a floured board. Knead it 10 times and only 10 times. Roll the dough flat, about 1/2 inch thick. Cut out round circles using a biscuit cutter or an overturned glass. Place the circles on a baking sheet. Do not let the circles touch one another. Bake at 350° for 10 to 12 minutes or until the biscuits are light brown on top. Serve them with butter and honey.

Forget about braided coffee cakes, cream-filled doughnuts, and giant muffins. When the water boils for your morning tea and you are looking for something to go with it, grab a fresh, hot biscuit.

Words to Write

What is your favorite breakfast food? Write the directions for how to make it. Be sure to include the ingredients and the steps. Use words from the Words to Know list.

Jalapeño Bagels

by Natasha Wing
illustrated by Antonio L. Castro

Genre

Realistic fiction is a made-up story that can be set in a real place. What is the setting of this story?

225

"**W**hat should I bring to school on Monday for International Day?" I ask my mother. "My teacher told us to bring something from our culture."

"You can bring a treat from the *panaderia*," she suggests. Panaderia is what Mama calls our bakery. "Help us bake on Sunday—then you can pick out whatever you want."

"It's a deal," I tell her. I like helping at the bakery. It's warm there, and everything smells so good.

Early Sunday morning, when it is still dark, my mother wakes me up.

"Pablo, it's time to go to work," she says.

We walk down the street to the bakery. My father turns
on the lights. My mother turns on the ovens. She gets
out the pans and ingredients for *pan dulce*. Pan dulce is
Mexican sweet bread.

I help my mother mix and knead the dough. She shapes
rolls and loaves of bread and slides them into the oven.
People tell her she makes the best pan dulce in town.

"Maybe I'll bring pan dulce to school," I tell her.

Next we make *empanadas de calabaza*—pumpkin turnovers. I'm in charge of spooning the pumpkin filling. Mama folds the dough in half and presses the edges with a fork. She bakes them until they are flaky and golden brown. Some customers come to our bakery just for her turnovers.

"Maybe I'll bring empanadas de calabaza instead."
"You'll figure it out," she says. "Ready to make
chango bars?" Chango means "monkey man."

Mama lets me pour in the chocolate chips and nuts.
When she's not looking, I pour in more chocolate chips.
"I could bring chango bars. They're my favorite dessert."
"Mine, too," says Mama. "This batch should be
especially good. I put in extra chips."

My father calls from the back room. "Pablo! Come help me with the bagels!" Papa speaks English and Yiddish. He learned Yiddish from his family in New York City. I know some words too. *Bubbe* means "grandmother." He uses my bubbe's recipe to make the bagels.

First he makes the dough in a big metal bowl. Then he rolls it out into a long rope shape. He cuts off pieces and shows me how to connect the ends in a circle. We put the circles on trays where they sit and rise.

231

While we are waiting my father makes *challah*, Jewish braided bread. He lets me practice braiding challah dough at my own counter. It's a lot like braiding hair. The customers say it is almost too beautiful to eat.

"Maybe I'll bring a loaf of challah to school," I tell Papa. He smiles.

When the bagel dough has risen, he boils the bagels in a huge pot of water and fishes them out with a long slotted spoon. I sprinkle on poppy seeds and sesame seeds, and then they go in the oven.

"Maybe I could bring sesame-seed bagels with cream cheese."

"No *lox?*" Lox is smoked salmon. My father's favorite bagel is pumpernickel with a smear of cream cheese and lox.

I crinkle my nose. "Lox tastes like fish. Jam is better."

My mother joins us and helps my father make another batch of bagels—*jalapeño* bagels. My parents use their own special recipe. While Papa kneads the dough, Mama chops the jalapeño *chiles*. She tosses them into the dough and adds dried red peppers. We roll, cut, make circles, and let them rise. I can't wait until they are done because I am getting hungry.

"Have you decided what you're going to bring to school?" asks Mama.

"It's hard to choose. Everything is so good," I tell her. I look at Papa. "Except for lox."

"You should decide before we open," warns Mama, "or else our customers will buy everything up."

I walk past all the sweet breads, chango bars, and bagels.

I think about my mother and my father and all the different things they make in the bakery. And suddenly I know exactly what I'm going to bring.

"Jalapeño bagels," I tell my parents. "And I'll spread them with cream cheese and jam."

"Why jalapeño bagels?" asks Papa.

"Because they are a mixture of both of you. Just like me!"

For this recipe you will need lots of time.
But these bagels are worth the wait!
Ask an adult to help you.

Jalapeño Bagels

1 3/4 cups lukewarm water

1/2 teaspoon dry yeast

2 teaspoons salt

1 1/2 tablespoons sugar

5 to 6 cups flour

1/3 cup jalapeños, chopped

1/4 cup dried red peppers

Mix water, yeast, salt, and sugar. Add flour and jalapeños and mix into a ball. Knead for 10 to 12 minutes, adding more flour if necessary, until dough is stiff. Add red peppers and knead for 3 minutes. Let dough rest 10 minutes, then cut into 12 pieces with a knife.

Roll each piece of dough on a table to form long, cigarlike shapes. Then, for each of the twelve pieces, connect the two ends by overlapping them about 3/4 of an inch and rolling the ends together to make a ring shape. Make sure each joint is secure or it will come apart while boiling.

Cover with a damp towel and let rise 1 to 1 1/2 hours in a warm spot. In a large pot, bring 1 to 2 gallons of water to a rolling boil. Place bagels in boiling water and boil until they float (15 to 30 seconds). Remove with a slotted spoon and place on a lightly greased cookie sheet. Bake at 400 degrees for 10 to 15 minutes or until golden brown.

Note: A bakery uses dry malt instead of sugar, and high-gluten flour, which you may be able to get at a bakery or pizza parlor. For a milder bagel, reduce the quantities of the peppers.

Reader Response

Open for Discussion Take a tasting trip through Pablo's parents' bakery. Which foods will get your taste test? Why?

1. Pictures help the author by showing action. Find three pictures in the story that show action. Tell about the action in each picture. **Think Like an Author**

2. Is the family bakery successful? What details from the story support your answer? **Draw Conclusions**

3. Summarize this story for a friend. What do you think is the most important part? Why? **Summarize**

4. Imagine you are a food critic for the local newspaper. Write a review of Pablo's jalapeño bagels. Use words from the Words to Know list and from the story. **Vocabulary**

Look Back and Write Why does Pablo like to help at the bakery? Look back at page 226. Use details from the story to write two reasons.

Meet author **Natasha Wing on page 419 and** illustrator **Antonio L. Castro on page 422.**

238

Write Now

Answer a Question

Prompt

Jalapeño Bagels describes a boy whose parents work in a bakery.
Think about the question, "What work do you want to do when you grow up?"
Now write an answer to the question.

Writer states main idea in first sentence.

Strong supporting reasons provide focus on main idea.

Last sentence sums up main idea.

Student Model

When I grow up, I want to be a children's doctor. My doctor is friendly and funny. When I have an ear infection or another problem, she always knows what is wrong. She knows which medicines I should take to make me better.

I love science. I like learning about health and how to prevent illnesses. Doctors have to train for many years. That doesn't bother me because I like to work hard and learn new things. When I grow up, I want to help kids feel better like my doctor does.

Use the model to help you answer a question.

239

Expository Nonfiction

Genre

- **Expository nonfiction uses text and pictures to provide information.**

- **Expository nonfiction gives details and facts about a subject.**

Text Features

- **In this article, vivid photographs show the fruits, vegetables, and spices of Mexico.**

- **Sections of the article are labeled with headings to introduce the information.**

Link to Social Studies

Use the library or the Internet to learn about foods from other cultures. Create a poster telling about the foods you learned about.

Foods of Mexico
a Delicious Blend

From *Viva Mexico! The Foods* by George Ancona

Panza llena, corazón contento is an old Mexican proverb that means "a full belly makes for a happy heart." The foods of Mexico are a treat to see, smell, taste, and eat.

Native Foods

The early people of Mexico developed maize (corn) from a small wild plant. They grew many varieties of maize: white, red, yellow, black, and other color combinations.

Between rows of corn they planted tomatoes, beans, chiles, pumpkins, sweet potatoes, and squash. They also raised avocados and amaranth, a nutritious grain that was ground into flour for tortillas and bread. Fields and forests supplied fruits, peanuts, cacao (cocoa) beans, honey, and mushrooms.

Squash

Honey

Sweet potatoes

Tomatoes

Chayote

Guayaba

Peanuts

Amaranth

Chiles

Tuna

Nopal

Cacao beans

Beans

Jiotilla

Avocado

Draw Conclusions Draw a conclusion about the native foods of Mexico.

The Spanish Flavor

The Spanish who came to the New World brought their traditions with them. Over the centuries Spain had had many influences. From the Greeks, who colonized Spain in the fifth century B.C., the Spanish learned to grow olives, grapes, and chickpeas. From the Moors, who ruled their country for eight hundred years, they learned to plant spinach, eggplants, artichokes, watermelons, sugarcane, and lime, lemon, and orange trees.

Spanish ships called galleons sailed across the Pacific Ocean from Spanish colonies in Asia. They brought many foods and spices with them. Rice from Asia together with Mexico's native beans (*frijoles*) and tortillas became the staple food of Mexico. African slaves who were brought to New Spain also added their ways of cooking.

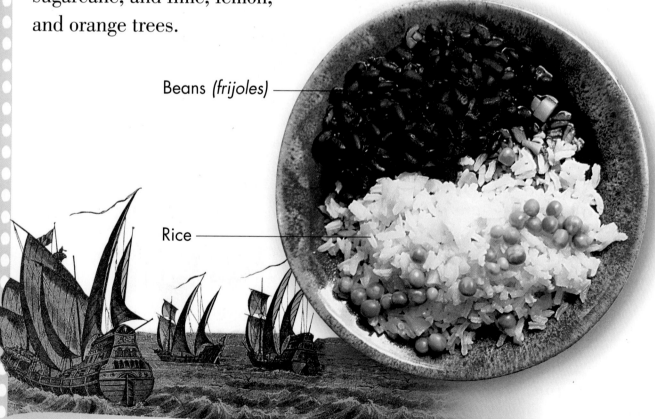

Beans (*frijoles*)

Rice

Tortillas o Bolillos?

The Spanish planted wheat because they preferred wheat bread to the native corn tortillas. They baked little rolls called *bolillos.* Serving *bolillos* was a status symbol among Europeans. But Mexicans never gave up their tortillas. Eventually the settlers began to eat them, too.

Today it isn't necessary to choose between a *tamale* or a *bolillo.* Street-corner food vendors sell a breakfast snack that blends two cultures: a sliced *bolillo* with a hot tamale inside. This is called a *torta de tamale,* a tamale sandwich.

Like seeds blown by the wind, people came to Mexico from distant lands, and they settled and flowered. The foods they brought with them blended with native cooking. The result is a Mexican cuisine that has traces of distant lands.

Tamales

Bolillos

Reading Across Texts
People came from distant lands to settle in Mexico. They blended their foods with the foods of the Mexican people. How did Pablo's family do something similar?

Writing Across Texts
Explain about a food you know that is a blend of two cultures.

 **Summarize** Summarize what you learned.

243

Author's Purpose

- The author's purpose is the reason an author has for writing.

- An author usually writes to inform, to persuade, to entertain, or to express an opinion.

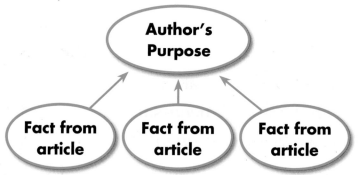

Strategy: Prior Knowledge

Good readers use what they already know to help them understand what they are reading. As you read, think about what you already know to help you understand why the author wrote something.

Write to Read

1. Read "New York City." Create a graphic organizer like the one above to determine the author's purpose.

2. Write a paragraph about the author's purposes for writing this piece. Then draw a picture of a place you have visited or seen on television that reminds you of New York City.

Have you ever been to New York City? It's a terrific place to visit. There are many things to see and do. New York City is the largest city in the United States.

Do you like interesting places? In New York City you can visit the Empire State Building. This grand building opened in 1931. It is 102 stories tall! For many years, it was the tallest building in the world.

Strategy What do you already know about New York City? How does that help you better understand what you just read?

Another breathtaking place is the Statue of Liberty. This statue stands on Bedloe's Island in New York Harbor. It was a gift from France in 1886. The Statue of Liberty rises to over 300 feet tall. People come from all over the world to see this famous statue.

If you enjoy great plays and musical events, Broadway, a street in the center of New York City, has it all. This is the most famous theater district in the country.

Skill Here you can think about why the author wrote this. Do you think it was to give you information about New York City?

There are many things to see and do in New York City. You will have a wonderful time when you come to visit!

Words to Know

flights

stoops

pitcher

ruined

fierce

treasure

feast

cardboard

Remember

Try the strategy. Then, if you need more help, use your glossary or a dictionary.

Vocabulary Strategy
for Homonyms

Context Clues When you read, you may come to a familiar word, but it doesn't make sense in the sentence. The word could be a homonym. Homonyms are words that are spelled the same but have different meanings. For example, *saw* means "looked at." *Saw* also means "a tool for cutting." Use the context—the words and sentences around the word—to figure out the correct meaning.

1. Reread the words and sentences around the word. Look for clues to the word's meaning.

2. Draw a conclusion about another meaning for the word.

3. Try the meaning in the sentence. Does it make sense?

Read "A Different Treasure Hunt." Look for words that are homonyms. Use context clues to figure out their meanings.

A DIFFERENT TREASURE HUNT

The summer I turned eight, my family moved from New York City to North Carolina. In the city, we climbed four flights of stairs to our apartment. The street was lined with apartment buildings, and people sat on their front stoops and listened to the noise. In North Carolina, we lived in a house. All the houses had front porches and yards. At night it was very dark and quiet.

In New York City, I was the best pitcher on the neighborhood baseball team. In North Carolina, I couldn't find enough kids my age for a team.

I thought my life was ruined. My mother saw my fierce face. She suggested I have a treasure hunt, but instead of looking for gold, I should look for baseball players. She promised to help by preparing a feast with all my favorite foods. I made signs on cardboard and posted them at the grocery store, the library, and the post office. The signs said:

I'm looking for baseball players.
Come to 124 Montgomery Street
June 28, 2:00 P.M.
FREE FOOD!

Do you think anyone showed up?

Words to Write

Answer the writer's question. Give reasons for your answer. Use as many words from the Words to Know list as you can.

Genre **Realistic fiction** is a made-up story that could actually happen. What events in this selection seem real?

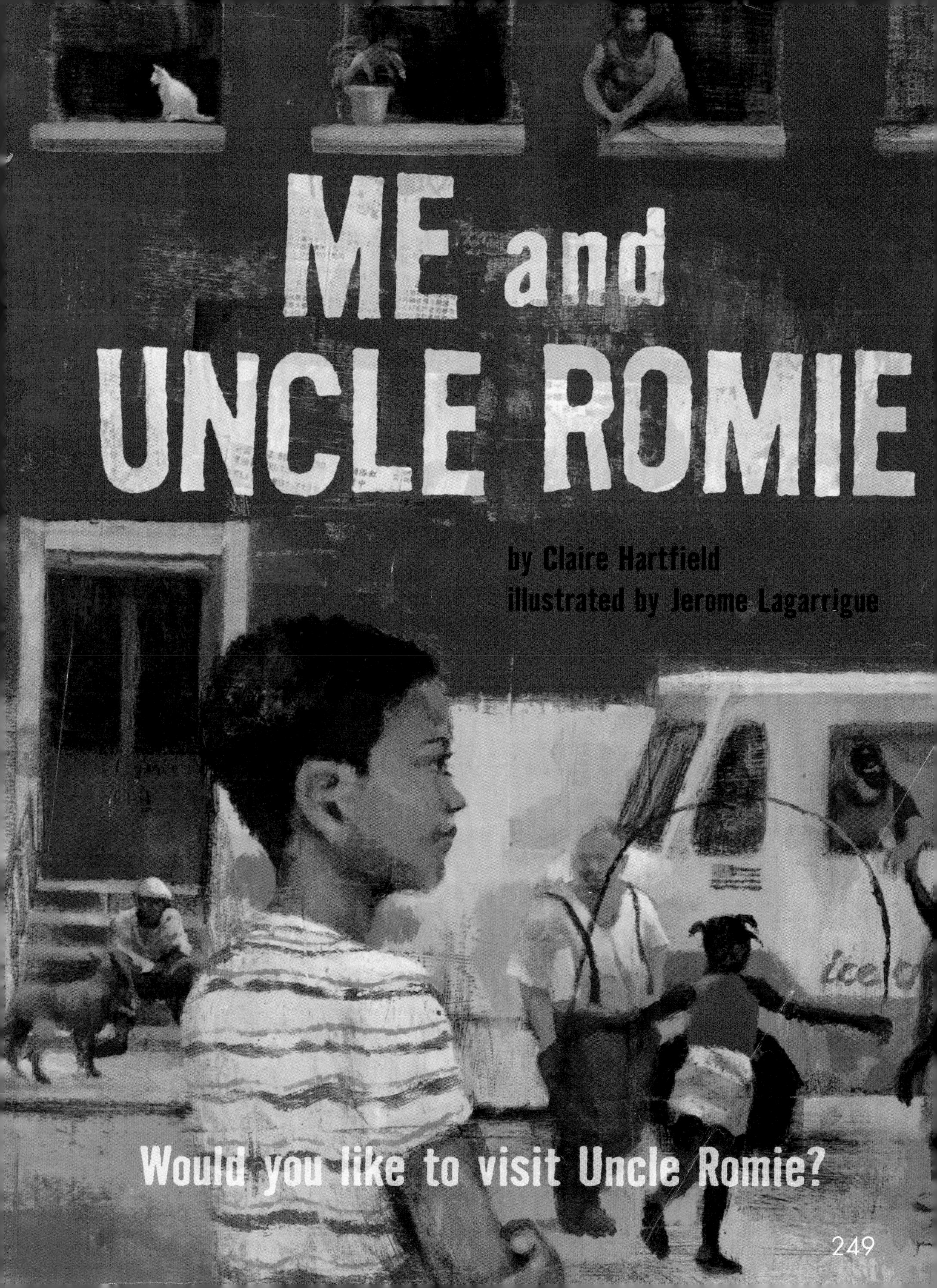

ME and UNCLE ROMIE

by Claire Hartfield
illustrated by Jerome Lagarrigue

Would you like to visit Uncle Romie?

It was the summer Mama had the twins that I first met my uncle Romie. The doctor had told Mama she had to stay off her feet till the babies got born. Daddy thought it was a good time for me to visit Uncle Romie and his wife, Aunt Nanette, up north in New York City. But I wasn't so sure. Mama had told me that Uncle Romie was some kind of artist, and he didn't have any kids. I'd seen his picture too. He looked scary—a bald-headed, fierce-eyed giant. No, I wasn't sure about this visit at all.

he day before I left home was a regular North Carolina summer day. "A good train-watching day," my friend B. J. said.

We waited quietly in the grass beside the tracks. B. J. heard it first. "It's a'coming," he said. Then I heard it too—a low rumbling, building to a roar. *WHOOO—OOO!*

"The *Piedmont!*" we shouted as the train blasted past.

"I'm the greatest train-watcher ever," B. J. boasted.

"Yeah," I answered, "but tomorrow I'll be *riding* a train. I'm the lucky one."

Lucky, I thought as we headed home. *Maybe.*

That evening I packed my suitcase. Voices drifted up from the porch below.

"Romie's got that big art show coming up," Mama said quietly. "I hope he's not too busy for James, especially on his birthday."

"Romie's a good man," Daddy replied. "And Nanette'll be there too."

The light faded. Mama called me into her bedroom. "Where's my good-night kiss?" she said.

I curled up next to her. "I'll miss the way you make my birthday special, Mama. Your lemon cake and the baseball game."

"Well," Mama sighed, "it won't be those things. But Uncle Romie and Aunt Nanette are family, and they love you too. It'll still be a good birthday, honey."

Mama pulled me close. Her voice sang soft and low. Later, in my own bed, I listened as crickets began their song and continued into the night.

The next morning I hugged Mama good-bye, and Daddy and I headed for the train. He got me seated, then stood waving at me from the outside. I held tight to the jar of pepper jelly Mama had given me for Uncle Romie.

"ALL A-BOARD!" The conductor's voice crackled over the loudspeaker.

The train pulled away. *Chug-a-chug-a-chug-a-chug.* I watched my town move past my window—bright-colored houses, chickens strutting across the yards, flowers everywhere.

After a while I felt hungry. Daddy had packed me
a lunch and a dinner to eat one at a time. I ate almost
everything at once. Then my belly felt tight and I was
kind of sleepy. I closed my eyes and dreamed about
Mama and Daddy getting ready for those babies. Would
they even miss me?

Later, when I woke up, I ate the last bit of my dinner
and thought about my birthday. Would they make my
lemon cake and take me to a baseball game in New York?

The sky turned from dark blue to black. I was
getting sleepy all over again.

"We're almost there, son," the man next to me said.

Then I saw it . . . New York City. Buildings stretching up
to the sky. So close together. Not like North Carolina at all.

"Penn Station! Watch your step," the conductor said, helping me down to the platform. I did like Daddy said and found a spot for myself close to the train. Swarms of people rushed by. Soon I heard a silvery voice call my name. This had to be Aunt Nanette. I turned and saw her big smile reaching out to welcome me.

She took my hand and guided me through the rushing crowds onto an underground train called the subway. "This will take us right home," she explained.

Home was like nothing I'd ever seen before. No
regular houses anywhere. Just big buildings and stores
of all kinds—in the windows I saw paints, fabrics,
radios, and TVs.

We turned into the corner building and climbed the
stairs to the apartment—five whole flights up. *Whew!*
I tried to catch my breath while Aunt Nanette flicked
on the lights.

"Uncle Romie's out talking to some people about
his big art show that's coming up. He'll be home soon,"
Aunt Nanette said. She set some milk and a plate of
cookies for me on the table. "Your uncle's working
very hard, so we won't see much of him for a while.
His workroom—we call it his studio—is in the front of
our apartment. That's where he keeps all the things he
needs to make his art."

"Doesn't he just paint?" I asked.

"Uncle Romie is a collage artist," Aunt Nanette explained. "He uses paints, yes. But also photographs, newspapers, cloth. He cuts and pastes them onto a board to make his paintings."

"That sounds kinda easy," I said.

Aunt Nanette laughed.

"Well, there's a little more to it than that, James. When you see the paintings, you'll understand. Come, let's get you to bed."

Lying in the dark, I heard heavy footsteps in the hall. A giant stared at me from the doorway. "Hello there, James." Uncle Romie's voice was deep and loud, like thunder. "Thanks for the pepper jelly," he boomed. "You have a good sleep, now." Then he disappeared down the hall.

The next morning the door to Uncle Romie's studio was closed. But Aunt Nanette had plans for both of us. "Today we're going to a neighborhood called Harlem," she said. "It's where Uncle Romie lived as a boy."

Harlem was full of people walking, working, shopping, eating. Some were watching the goings-on from fire escapes. Others were sitting out on stoops greeting folks who passed by—just like the people back home calling out hellos from their front porches. Most everybody seemed to know Aunt Nanette. A lot of them asked after Uncle Romie too.

We bought peaches at the market, then stopped to visit awhile. I watched some kids playing stickball. "Go on, get in that game," Aunt Nanette said, gently pushing me over to join them. When I was all hot and sweaty, we cooled off with double chocolate scoops from the ice cream man. Later we shared some barbecue on a rooftop way up high. I felt like I was on top of the world.

As the days went by, Aunt Nanette took me all over the city—we rode a ferry boat to the Statue of Liberty . . . zoomed 102 floors up at the Empire State Building . . . window-shopped the fancy stores on Fifth Avenue . . . gobbled hot dogs in Central Park.

But it was Harlem that I liked best. I played stickball with the kids again . . . and on a really hot day a whole bunch of us ran through the icy cold water that sprayed out hard from the fire hydrant. In the evenings Aunt Nanette and I sat outside listening to the street musicians playing their saxophone songs.

259

On rainy days I wrote postcards and helped out around the apartment. I told Aunt Nanette about the things I liked to do back home—about baseball games, train-watching, my birthday. She told me about the special Caribbean lemon and mango cake she was going to make.

My uncle Romie stayed hidden away in his studio. But I wasn't worried anymore. Aunt Nanette would make my birthday special.

4 . . . 3 . . . 2 . . . 1 . . . My birthday was almost here!

And then Aunt Nanette got a phone call.

"An old aunt has died, James. I have to go away for her funeral. But don't you worry. Uncle Romie will spend your birthday with you. It'll be just fine."

That night Aunt Nanette kissed me good-bye. I knew it would not be fine at all. Uncle Romie didn't know about cakes or baseball games or anything except his dumb old paintings. My birthday was ruined.

When the sky turned black, I tucked myself into bed. I missed Mama and Daddy so much. I listened to the birds on the rooftop—their songs continued into the night.

The next morning everything was quiet. I crept out of bed and into the hall. For the first time the door to Uncle Romie's studio stood wide open. What a glorious mess! There were paints and scraps all over the floor, and around the edges were huge paintings with all sorts of pieces pasted together.

I saw saxophones, birds, fire escapes, and brown faces. *It's Harlem,* I thought. *The people, the music, the rooftops, and the stoops.* Looking at Uncle Romie's paintings, I could *feel* Harlem—its beat and bounce.

Then there was one that was different. Smaller houses, flowers, and trains. "That's home!" I shouted.

"Yep," Uncle Romie said, smiling, from the doorway. "That's the Carolina I remember."

"Mama says you visited your grandparents there most every summer when you were a kid," I said.

"I sure did, James. *Mmm.* Now that's the place for pepper jelly. Smeared thick on biscuits. And when Grandma wasn't looking . . . I'd sneak some on a spoon."

"Daddy and I do that too!" I told him.

We laughed together, then walked to the kitchen for a breakfast feast—eggs, bacon, grits, and biscuits.

"James, you've got me remembering the pepper jelly lady. People used to line up down the block to buy her preserves."

"Could you put someone like that in one of your paintings?" I asked.

"I guess I could." Uncle Romie nodded. "Yes, that's a memory just right for sharing. What a good idea, James. Now let's get this birthday going!"

He brought out two presents from home. I tore into the packages while he got down the pepper jelly and two huge spoons. Mama and Daddy had picked out just what I wanted—a special case for my baseball cards, and a model train for me to build.

"Pretty cool," said Uncle Romie. "I used to watch the trains down in North Carolina, you know."

How funny to picture big Uncle Romie lying on his belly!

"B. J. and me, we have contests to see who can hear the trains first."

"Hey, I did that too. You know, it's a funny thing, James. People live in all sorts of different places and families. But the things we care about are pretty much the same. Like favorite foods, special songs, games, stories . . . and like birthdays." Uncle Romie held up two tickets to a baseball game!

It turns out Uncle Romie knows all about baseball—he was even a star pitcher in college. We got our mitts and set off for the game.

Way up in the bleachers, we shared a bag of peanuts, cracking the shells with our teeth and keeping our mitts ready in case a home run ball came our way. That didn't happen—but we sure had fun.

Aunt Nanette came home that night. She lit the candles, and we all shared my Caribbean birthday cake.

After that, Uncle Romie had to work a lot again. But at the end of each day he let me sit with him in his studio and talk. Daddy was right. Uncle Romie is a good man.

The day of the big art show finally came. I watched the people laughing and talking, walking slowly around the room from painting to painting. I walked around myself, listening to their conversations.

"Remember our first train ride from Chicago to New York?" one lady asked her husband.

"That guitar-playing man reminds me of my Uncle Joe," said another.

All these strangers talking to each other about their families and friends and special times, and all because of how my uncle Romie's paintings reminded them of these things.

Later that night Daddy called. I had a brand-new brother and sister. Daddy said they were both bald and made a lot of noise. But he sounded happy and said how they all missed me.

This time Aunt Nanette and Uncle Romie took me to the train station.

"Here's a late birthday present for you, James," Uncle Romie said, holding out a package. "Open it on the train, why don't you. It'll help pass the time on the long ride home."

I waved out the window to Uncle Romie and Aunt Nanette until I couldn't see them anymore. Then I ripped off the wrappings!

And there was my summer in New York. Bright sky in one corner, city lights at night in another. Tall buildings. Baseball ticket stubs. The label from the pepper-jelly jar. And trains. One going toward the skyscrapers. Another going away.

Back home, I lay in the soft North Carolina grass. It was the first of September, almost Uncle Romie's birthday. I watched the birds streak across the sky.

Rooftop birds, I thought. *Back home from their summer in New York, just like me.* Watching them, I could still feel the city's beat inside my head.

A feather drifted down from the sky. In the garden tiger lilies bent in the wind. *Uncle Romie's favorite flowers.* I yanked off a few blossoms. And then I was off on a treasure hunt, collecting things that reminded me of Uncle Romie.

I painted and pasted them together on a big piece of cardboard. Right in the middle I put the train schedule. And at the top I wrote:

Reader Response

Open for Discussion Help James answer three questions from folks back home: "How was your visit? How homesick were you? How did Uncle Romie manage to find time for you?"

1. It would be more polite to name this story *Uncle Romie and I*. Why did the author name it *Me and Uncle Romie* instead? **Think Like an Author**

2. Look carefully at the illustrations. Using what you know about the story, why did the illustrator choose this style of art? **Author's Purpose**

3. What do you know or what have you read about cities? How did that help you as you read this story? **Prior Knowledge**

4. We know that James wrote postcards from New York City to his family in North Carolina. Write a message that he might have sent. Use words from the Words to Know list and from the story. **Vocabulary**

Look Back and Write Look back at pages 268 and 269. Tell what was special about the birthday gift James made for Uncle Romie.

Meet author **Claire Hartfield on page 418 and** illustrator **Jerome Lagarrigue on page 423.**

Write Now

Story Review

Prompt

In *Me and Uncle Romie*, Uncle Romie says everyone has special stories that he or she loves.

Think about a story that is special to you. Now write a story review telling why readers should read the story.

Student Model

No mistakes in <u>conventions</u> makes writing easier to read.

Writer describes story's plot but doesn't retell whole story.

Writer relates story to readers.

> Good-Bye, 382 Shin Dang Dong is a special story. The main character is a girl who has to move with her family from Korea to America. She feels sad to leave her house, her room, and her best friend. However, when she gets to the United States, she finds that she likes her new room, house, and friends too. Many kids have had to move to a new place. This story will help them remember and understand their feelings about moving.

Use the model to help you write your own story review.

Online Reference Sources

Genre

- **You can find reference sources, such as atlases, dictionaries, and encyclopedias on Internet Web sites.**

- **Some Web sites give you several different reference sources all in one place.**

Text Features

- **These reference sources look a lot like printed sources, and they're organized the same way.**

Link to Art

Find examples of art forms in newspapers, magazines, and books. Bring examples of your favorites to class.

Country to City

Denise learned a little about Romare Bearden from reading *Me and Uncle Romie*. She was curious to learn more about his life in the country and in the city. She wondered how the cultures were different.

Denise knew that she could look up information about Romare Bearden in an encyclopedia, but she didn't have one handy.

For more practice

Take It to the Net

PearsonSuccessNet.com

She remembered seeing a link to online reference sources when she was on the Internet. It had links to an atlas, almanac, dictionary, and encyclopedia.

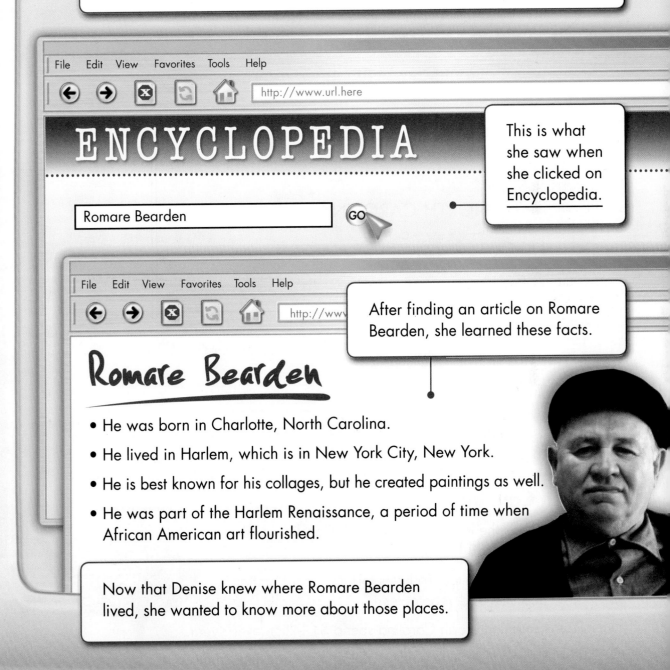

File   Edit   View   Favorites   Tools   Help

http://www.url.here

ENCYCLOPEDIA

Romare Bearden

GO

This is what she saw when she clicked on Encyclopedia.

File   Edit   View   Favorites   Tools   Help

http://www

Romare Bearden

After finding an article on Romare Bearden, she learned these facts.

- He was born in Charlotte, North Carolina.
- He lived in Harlem, which is in New York City, New York.
- He is best known for his collages, but he created paintings as well.
- He was part of the Harlem Renaissance, a period of time when African American art flourished.

Now that Denise knew where Romare Bearden lived, she wanted to know more about those places.

Prior Knowledge   What do you already know about Romare Bearden?

Denise used the atlas to find a map of North Carolina.

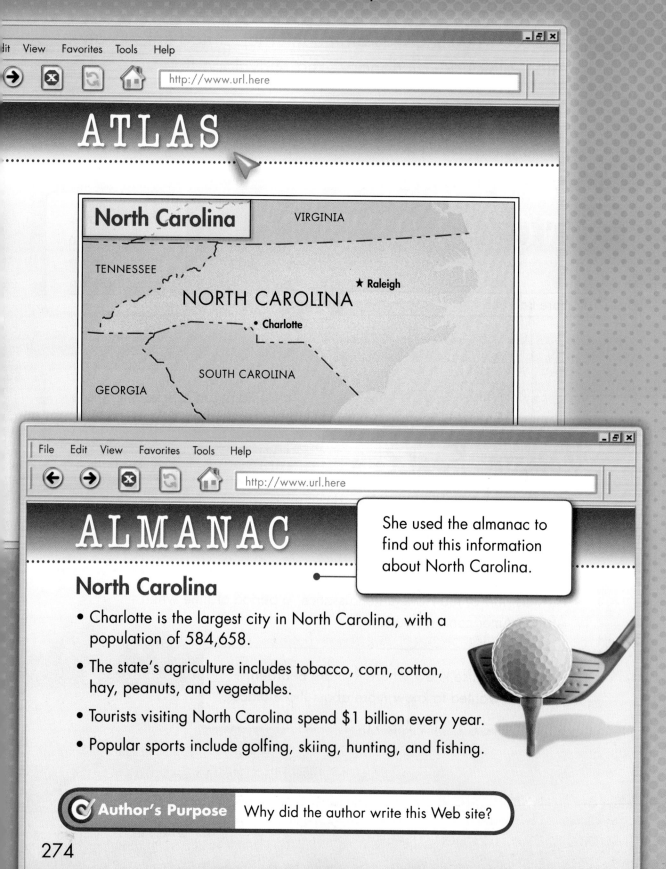

View Favorites Tools Help

http://www.url.here

ATLAS

North Carolina

VIRGINIA

TENNESSEE

NORTH CAROLINA   ★ Raleigh

• Charlotte

SOUTH CAROLINA

GEORGIA

File Edit View Favorites Tools Help

http://www.url.here

ALMANAC

She used the almanac to find out this information about North Carolina.

North Carolina

- Charlotte is the largest city in North Carolina, with a population of 584,658.

- The state's agriculture includes tobacco, corn, cotton, hay, peanuts, and vegetables.

- Tourists visiting North Carolina spend $1 billion every year.

- Popular sports include golfing, skiing, hunting, and fishing.

Author's Purpose Why did the author write this Web site?

ATLAS

Then Denise used the atlas to find a map of New York.

The almanac gave her some facts about the state of New York. Denise looked at the information she had gathered and saw some differences between the two places Romare Bearden had lived in.

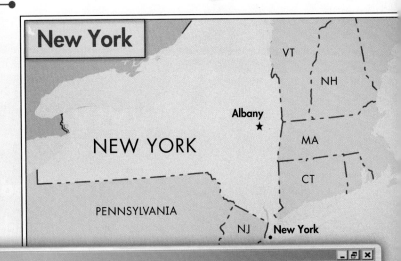

New York

VT
NH
Albany ★
NEW YORK
MA
CT
PENNSYLVANIA
NJ New York

http://www.url.here

ALMANAC

New York

- The largest city in the state is New York City, which has a population of 8,085,742.

- New York City is a leader in manufacturing, banking, and book publishing.

- New York City is a popular travel destination in the state of New York.

- The state produces grapes, strawberries, cherries, pears, onions, potatoes, and dairy products.

Reading Across Texts

What information about the city and the country can you get from *Me and Uncle Romie* that you don't get from this Web site?

Writing Across Texts Make a chart listing information about the city and the country.

275

My Friend in School

by Tony Medina

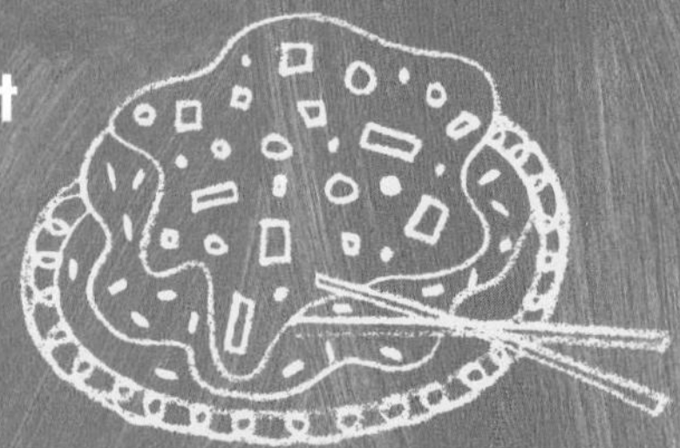

My friend in school
is Johnny Tse
you say it like
the letter C
he's Chinese
I like that 'cause I learn
new things from him
like different foods to eat
new words to speak
and—oh yeah—
    karate!
which is Japanese—not Chinese
and I don't like it too much
'cause you gotta kick real high
but I like the clothes
you have to wear

I go over to his house
to play video games
he comes over to my house
to eat and to watch cartoons

My friend in school
is Johnny Tse
which sounds like C
or see or sea
or sí (that's Spanish
if you didn't know)

My friend in school
is Johnny Tse
he's Chinese
and likes to sneeze
and when he does that
in school or outside
we laugh and laugh
and people wonder what
and wonder why and
what's so funny all the time

Lunch Survey

by Kristine O'Connell George

We open our paper bags:

Peanut butter plain
Peanut butter tortilla
Peanut butter pita
P B & J
P B & mayo
P B & banana
P B & pickles

Zach lifts the lid of his
insulated aluminum lunch box:
sushi.

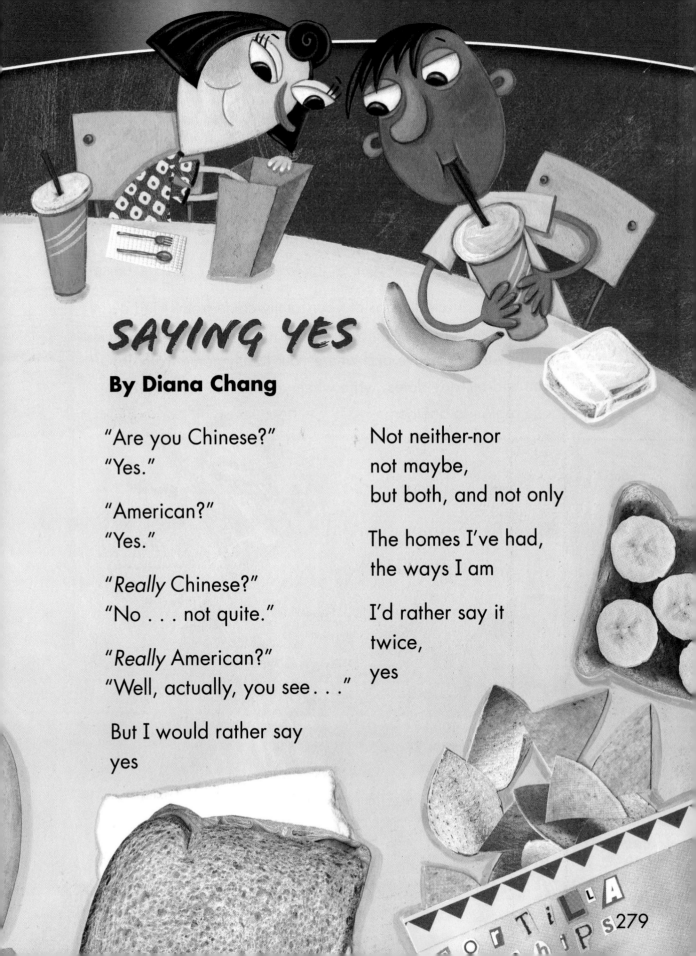

SAYING YES

By Diana Chang

"Are you Chinese?"
"Yes."

"American?"
"Yes."

"*Really* Chinese?"
"No . . . not quite."

"*Really* American?"
"Well, actually, you see. . ."

But I would rather say
yes

Not neither-nor
not maybe,
but both, and not only

The homes I've had,
the ways I am

I'd rather say it
twice,
yes

WRAP-UP

Finding My Roots

Where do different parts of your family come from? Find out where some of your relatives were born. Then make a map. Show where you live and where your family came from. If you find out any dates, write when your family moved from one region to another.

What happens when two ways of life come together?

BUBBLE

North and South

connect to
WRITING

In *Me and Uncle Romie,* James discovers how different life in Harlem is from life in the South. Pretend you are James. Write a letter home to tell your family about your experiences in New York.

Dear Mom and Dad,

Part of My Culture

connect to
SOCIAL STUDIES

Ask your family about a part of your heritage that is shown in your food, dress, art, crafts, music, or some other form of culture. Make a picture, learn a song or dance, or find another way that you can share this part of your culture with your class.

How to make Challah

3/4 cup warm water
2 eggs (large)
1/3 cup white sugar
1/3 cup canola oil

UNIT 6

Read It Online
PearsonSuccessNet.com

Freedom

What does it mean to be free?

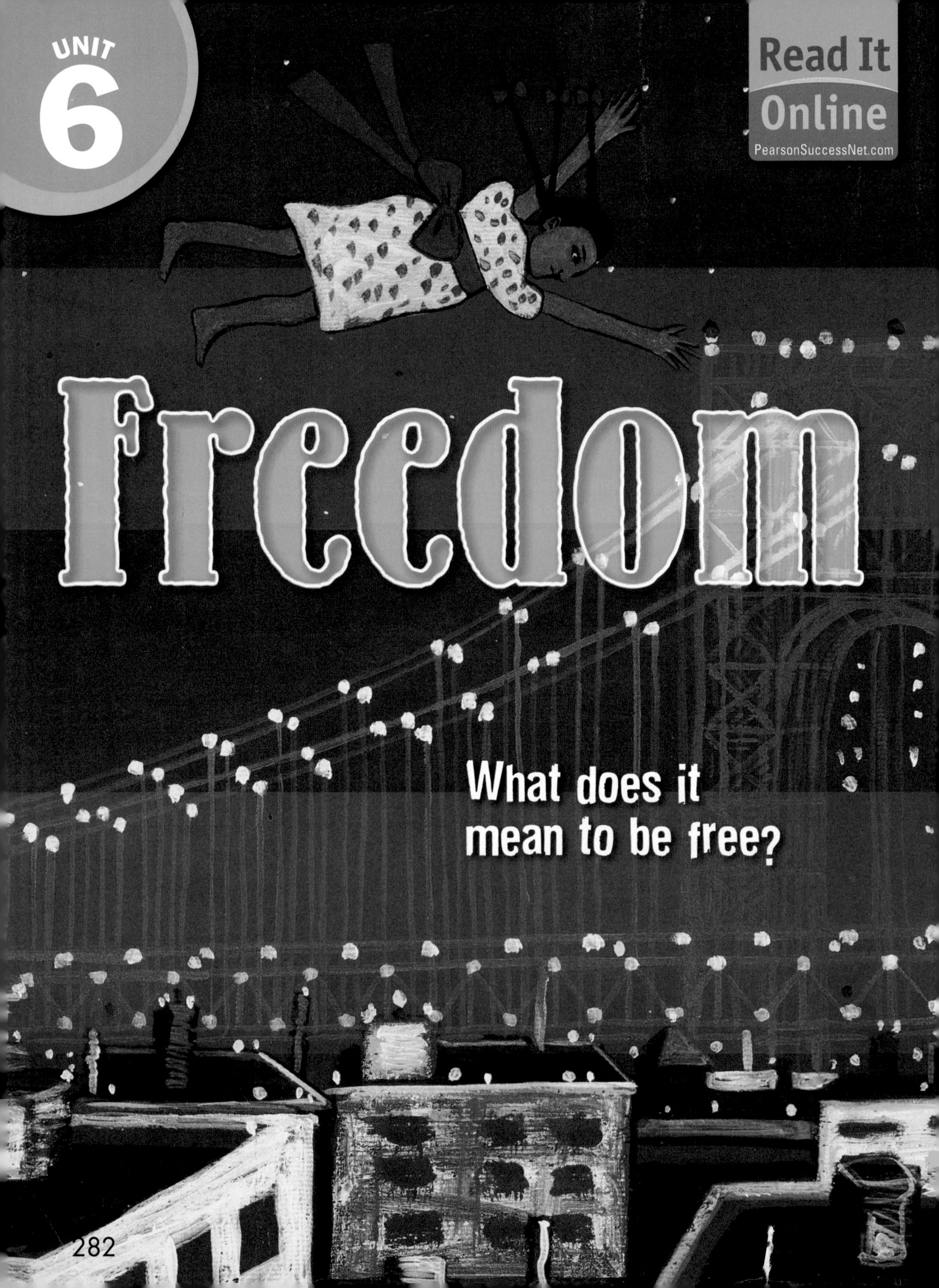

The Story of the Statue of Liberty
The Statue of Liberty has come to symbolize American freedom.

NARRATIVE NONFICTION

connect to SOCIAL STUDIES

Happy Birthday Mr. Kang
Mr. Kang makes an important decision about his pet bird.

REALISTIC FICTION

connect to SCIENCE

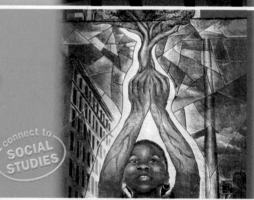

Talking Walls: Art for the People
Artists express freedom through murals.

PHOTO ESSAY

connect to SOCIAL STUDIES

Two Bad Ants
Ants learn the difficulties of a free life.

ANIMAL FANTASY

connect to SCIENCE

Elena's Serenade
Elena learns she has the freedom to follow her dream.

FANTASY

connect to SOCIAL STUDIES

283

The Story of the Statue of Liberty

Comprehension

Skill
Main Idea
and Details

Strategy
Text Structure

Skill

Main Idea and Details

- The main idea is the most important idea in a selection or a paragraph.

- The small pieces of information that tell about the main idea are the supporting details.

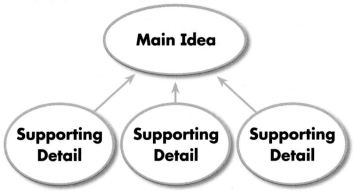

Main Idea

Supporting Detail

Supporting Detail

Supporting Detail

Strategy

Strategy: Text Structure

Active readers think about how a selection is organized and written. It's a good idea to look for key words in the text, such as *who, what, where, why,* and *when.* These key words will give you details about the main idea.

Write to Read

1. Read "Coming to America." Then make a graphic organizer like the one above to show the main idea and details.

2. Write a paragraph about where your ancestors came from.

Coming to America

The country where you were born is called your *homeland*. People who leave their homeland and come to another country—such as America—are called *immigrants*. America has been called a "Nation of Immigrants." Why? ●——

Strategy Here is a key word—*why*—that gives you a clue. The next part of this selection will probably answer that question.

Everyone who lives in America now (except for Native Americans) once came from somewhere else. This may have happened a very long time ago in your family. Maybe the ones to come to America were your great-great-great-great-great grandparents. Or maybe you and your family arrived here recently.

Immigrants leave their homeland for ●—— different reasons. Some came to America looking for religious freedom. Some came to escape war or hunger. Others came for adventure. But mostly, people came looking for a better life for themselves and their children.

Skill Here is the main idea of this paragraph—people came to America for many reasons. Now read on to find the supporting details.

The next time you have a coin, turn it over and look for the motto of the United States on the back. The words are in Latin, and they say *E pluribus unum*. They mean "Out of many, one."

People came to America from all over the world, but together, we are one nation!

The Story of the Statue of Liberty

Words to Know

liberty

unveiled

crown

torch

tablet

models

symbol

unforgettable

Remember

Try the strategy. Then, if you need more help, use your glossary or a dictionary.

Vocabulary Strategy
for Prefixes

Word Structure When you see a word you don't know, look closely at the word. Does it have *un-* at the beginning? The prefix *un-* makes the word mean "not ____" or "the opposite of ____." For example, *unhappy* means "not happy." You can use the prefix to help you figure out the meaning of the word.

1. Put your finger over *un-*.

2. Look at the base word. Put the base word in the phrase "not ____" or "the opposite of ____."

3. Try that meaning in the sentence. Does it make sense?

Read "Emma and Liberty." Look for words that begin with *un-*. Use the prefix to help you figure out the meanings of the words.

Emma and Liberty

Emma is visiting New York City. What she wants to see more than anything else is the Statue of Liberty. Emma knows everything about Liberty. She knows why the statue was made, who made it, and when it was unveiled in New York Harbor. She knows how tall it is from its base to its crown, what its torch is made of, and what is written on the tablet. Emma has collected pictures of the statue and made models of it. However, she has never seen the real Liberty.

From Battery Park in lower Manhattan, Emma can see the Statue of Liberty in the distance. She waits in line for the boat that will take her to the island. As the boat gets nearer, Emma imagines what it was like for the immigrants who sailed past Liberty as they arrived in America. At last Emma is standing at Liberty's feet. She tilts her head back to look up at this symbol of freedom. It is an unforgettable moment.

Words to Write

What do you know about the Statue of Liberty or another symbol of America? Write about it. Use as many words from the Words to Know list as you can.

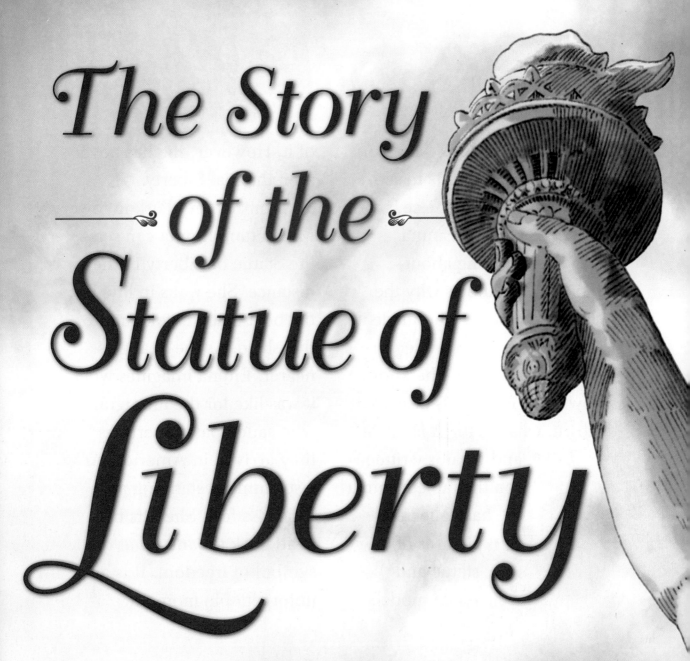

The Story
of the
Statue of
Liberty

by Betsy & Giulio Maestro

Genre

Narrative nonfiction gives information about real people and events in the form of a story. What special event does this selection tell about?

288

The Statue of Liberty stands on an island in New York Harbor. She is a beautiful sight to all who pass by her. Each year, millions of visitors ride the ferry out to the island. They climb to the top of the statue and enjoy the lovely view.

A young French sculptor named Frédéric Auguste Bartholdi visited America in 1871. When he saw Bedloe's Island in New York Harbor, he knew it was just the right place for a statue he wanted to build.

Bartholdi had created many other statues and monuments, but this one was to be very special. It was to be a present from the people of France to the people of America, as a remembrance of the old friendship between the two countries.

When Bartholdi got back to Paris, he made sketches and some small models. The statue would be a woman whom he would call Liberty. She would be a symbol of the freedom in the New World. She would hold a lamp in her raised hand to welcome people who came to America. She would be *Liberty Enlightening the World.*

The statue would be very large and very strong. Bartholdi wanted people to be able to climb up inside the statue and look out over the harbor from the crown and torch.

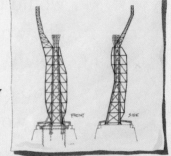

Many well-known artists, engineers, and craftsmen gave him ideas about how to build the statue. First, a huge skeleton was constructed from strong steel.

Many people worked together in a large workshop. Some worked on Liberty's head and crown. Others worked on her right hand, which would hold the torch.

In her left hand she would hold a tablet with the date July 4, 1776, written on it. This is when the Declaration of Independence was signed.

The arm holding the torch was sent to Philadelphia for America's 100th birthday celebration in 1876. Afterward, it stood in Madison Square in New York City for a number of years.

Liberty's head was shown at the World's Fair in Paris during this time. Visitors were able to climb inside and look around. In this way, money was raised to pay for the statue.

Then, skin of gleaming copper was put onto the skeleton and held in place with iron straps. As the huge statue grew, all of Paris watched with great fascination.

Finally, in 1884, Liberty was completed. There was a big celebration in Paris. Many famous people came to see her. Only a few had the energy to climb all the way to the crown—168 steps!

Then began the hard work of taking Liberty apart for the long voyage across the Atlantic Ocean. Each piece was marked and packed into a crate. There were 214 crates in all. They were carried by train and then put on a ship to America.

But in America people had lost interest in the Statue of Liberty. Money had run out and work on Bedloe's Island had stopped. The base for the statue was not finished. With the help of a large New York newspaper, the money was raised. People all over the country, including children, sent in whatever they could. By the time the ship reached New York in 1885, it was greeted with new excitement.

The work on the island went on, and soon the pedestal was completed. Piece by piece, the skeleton was raised. Then the copper skin was riveted in place. Liberty was put back together like a giant puzzle. The statue had been built not once, but twice!

At last, in 1886, Liberty was standing where she belonged. A wonderful celebration was held. Boats and ships filled the harbor. Speeches were read, songs were sung. Bartholdi himself unveiled Liberty's face and she stood, gleaming in all her glory, for everyone to see. There was a great cheer from the crowd. Then President Grover Cleveland gave a speech.

Over the years, immigrants have arrived to begin new lives in America. To them, the Statue of Liberty is a symbol of all their hopes and dreams. She has welcomed millions of people arriving in New York by ship.

Every year, on the Fourth of July, the United States of America celebrates its independence. Fireworks light up the sky above New York Harbor. The Statue of Liberty is a truly unforgettable sight—a symbol of all that is America.

"Give me your tired, your poor,
Your huddled masses yearning to breathe free,
The wretched refuse of your teeming shore.
Send these, the homeless, tempest-tost to me,
I lift my lamp beside the golden door!"

–from "The New Colossus" by Emma Lazarus, 1883, placed on
a tablet on the pedestal of the Statue of Liberty in 1903

Reader Response

Open for Discussion Every day in rain, snow, or sunshine the Statue of Liberty stands on her island. Why is she there? Why is she so famous?

1. The authors include details, such as the number of steps to the statue's crown. Why did they do that? Find other details. How do details help you know the Statue of Liberty? **Think Like an Author**

2. Building the Statue of Liberty was a complicated project. Look back at pages 292–295. What details support that fact? **Main Idea and Details**

3. This selection is told in the order in which events happened. What clue words did you notice that helped you recognize the sequential text structure? **Text Structure**

4. Imagine you have a pen pal who has never seen the Statue of Liberty, even in a picture. Write a description for your pen pal. Use words from the Words to Know list. **Vocabulary**

Look Back and Write What does the Statue of Liberty hold in her right hand and in her left hand? Look back at page 292. Why is that important?

Meet authors Betsy and Giulio Maestro on page 420.

Write Now

Take Notes

Prompt

The Story of the Statue of Liberty tells how a sculptor created this famous statue. Think about the most important ideas in the selection.

Now write notes about one part of the selection.

Writing Trait

Good writers **focus** on important **ideas** and support these ideas with strong details.

Student Model

Notes <u>focus</u> only on most important <u>ideas</u> in story.

Notes on The Story of The Statue of Liberty

French sculptor Frédéric Auguste Bartholdi
    visited America in 1871 and saw island in N.Y.

Decided to make statue as present from France
    S of L shows friendship between US and France
    S of L a symbol of freedom—welcomed people

She would be "Liberty Enlightening the World"
S of L large, strong—people could climb inside

Holds tablet with July 4, 1776

Arm with torch sent to Philadelphia, 1876

Liberty's head at Paris World's Fair—visitors paid to
    climb inside, raised $ for statue

Writer uses own words. Author's words are in quotation marks.

Notes are not always in complete sentences.

Use the model to help you write your own notes.

301

A Nation of Immigrants

Textbook

Genre

- A textbook is a source of information.

- A textbook can be about any subject taught in school.

Text Features

- Photos and captions make information clearer.

- Charts often are included to give additional information.

Link to Social Studies

Use the library or the Internet to find out more about why immigrants came to the United States. Copy the chart on page 303, and add a column that tells Why They Came.

Ellis Island

For decades, immigrants have come to the United States from almost every other country in the world. Some people wanted freedom or better opportunities. Some came because there was very little food in their home country. Some came to find jobs or to work on farms. Others came because they had no choice.

Many ships that came from Europe arrived first at Ellis Island in New York Harbor. Many immigrants from Asia arrived at Angel Island in San Francisco Bay. Immigrants also entered through other cities, such as Boston, Massachusetts; Galveston, Texas; and New Orleans, Louisiana.

★ ─────────────── ★

REVIEW What were some reasons immigrants came to the United States?

Times When Many Immigrants Came

Time Period	Where Many Were From
Before 1820	United Kingdom, countries of Western Africa such as those now known as Ghana, Togo, Benin, Nigeria, and Cameroon
1820–1860	Ireland, Germany, United Kingdom, France, Canada
1861–1890	Germany, United Kingdom, Ireland, Canada, Norway/Sweden
1891–1920	Italy, Austria/Hungary, Russia, United Kingdom, Germany
1961–1990	Mexico, Philippines, Canada, Korea, Cuba

Angel Island

Reading Across Texts

Immigrants from which countries would have been the first to see the new Statue of Liberty on Bedloe's Island?

Writing Across Texts Imagine that you are one of those immigrants. Write a journal entry telling your impression of the Statue of Liberty.

Main Idea What is the main idea of this article?

Comprehension

Skill
Cause and Effect

Strategy
Graphic
Organizers

 # Cause and Effect

- An effect is something that happens. A cause is why that thing happens.

- A cause may have more than one effect: *Because I forgot to set my alarm clock, I overslept, and I was late for school.*

- An effect may have more than one cause: *Dad's computer crashed because it didn't have enough memory, and he was running too many programs at once.*

Causes ⟶	Effects

Strategy: Graphic Organizers

A graphic organizer can help you identify and organize information as you read. You can make one like this and fill it in with causes and effects as you read the story.

Write to Read

1. Read "A New Life." Look for causes and effects in the story. Make a graphic organizer like the one above.

2. Fill in your chart as you read the story.

304

A New Life

"Thank you," said Mr. and Mrs. García, as the customer left the store. "Please come again."

The Garcías repeated these words many times every day, as a steady stream of customers entered and left their small grocery store. Business was good, and the García family was making a good living from the store. Still, at times they were sad because they missed their beautiful little village in northern Mexico. They also missed all of the family members they had left behind when they moved to Chicago.

"¡Hola!" shouted Rosa as she burst through the back door of the store. "I got my report card today. Here it is."

The Garcías looked at the report card and then hugged Rosa. She was doing so well in her new school! And the store was doing well too. They were happy. Yes, they missed their old home in Mexico. But here in Chicago, they had found a better life for themselves and for Rosa.

Skill The clue word *because* signals a cause. What causes the Garcías to be sad?

Strategy Here are some more causes and effects. If you made a graphic organizer, you could add this information to it.

narrow

foolish

perches

bows

recipe

chilly

foreign

Remember

Try the strategy. Then, if you need more help, use your glossary or a dictionary.

Vocabulary Strategy
for Antonyms

Context Clues Sometimes when you are reading, you will see a word you don't know. The words around it might help you figure out the meaning. For example, the author may give you an antonym for the word. An antonym is a word that means the opposite of another word. For example, *thin* is the opposite of *thick.* Look for another word that might be an antonym and see if it will help you figure out the meaning of the word you don't know.

1. Look at the words around the unfamiliar word. Perhaps the author used an antonym.

2. Look for words that seem to have opposite meanings. Think about the one word you know.

3. Use that word to help you figure out the meaning of its antonym.

As you read "Mr. Wang's Wonderful Noodles," look for antonyms to help you understand the meanings of the vocabulary words.

MR. WANG'S WONDERFUL Noodles

Mr. Wang is the best noodle maker in Shanghai, China. People who like wide, thick noodles may think people who like narrow, thin noodles are foolish. People who like narrow, thin noodles may think people who like wide, thick noodles are not very smart. But everyone agrees on one thing. Mr. Wang's noodles are the best.

When a customer comes to the noodle shop and perches on a stool at the counter, Mr. Wang always bows his head with respect, as if to say "Thank you for coming to my shop."

One day a stranger came into the noodle shop. He said, "Mr. Wang, please bring your noodle recipe to the United States. Make noodles in my restaurant."

The warm shop suddenly felt chilly. People stopped slurping their noodles to listen to Mr. Wang's reply.

Mr. Wang quietly said, "Thank you. But I do not wish to go to a foreign land. I am happy making noodles in China."

Everyone heaved a sigh of relief and went back to slurping Mr. Wang's wonderful noodles.

Words to Write

Write about your favorite food. How does it taste? Why do you like it? Use words from the Words to Know list.

HAPPY BIRTHDAY MR. KANG

WRITTEN AND ILLUSTRATED BY SUSAN L. ROTH

WHAT IS SPECIAL ABOUT
MR. KANG'S BIRTHDAY?

Forty-three years before his grandson, Sam, was born in the New World, Mr. Kang left China and came to America. Every day he chopped scallions, wrapped dumplings, and pulled noodle dough into long and perfect strands for the hungry people who ate at the Golden Dragon Restaurant in New York City.

When Mr. Kang turned seventy, Mrs. Kang had a birthday party for him.

"Make a wish!" said Sam as Mr. Kang shut his eyes, puffed his cheeks, and blew out all the candles on his cake. Everyone clapped and shouted hurray.

"What was your wish?" Sam asked.

"Three wishes," said Mr. Kang. "I want to read *The New York Times* every day. I want to paint poems every day. And I want a bird, a *hua mei*, of my own. I'll feed him every day, and on Sundays I'll take him to Sara Delano Roosevelt Park on Delancey Street. Enough cooking."

"Good idea," said Mrs. Kang. "I'll cook for you, and the Golden Dragon Restaurant can get a new cook."

"Grandpa, why do you want a bird in a cage? There are birds all over the place outside," said Sam.

"Sam," said Mr. Kang. "This is not just an American bird in a cage. This is a Chinese bird. My grandfather had a hua mei in a cage. Now I want a hua mei in a cage. And sometimes you and I will take him to Sara Delano Roosevelt Park on Delancey Street together."

And so it is that every morning Mr. Kang finds *The New York Times* on his doorstep. Every morning he reads it while he drinks his tea and eats his sweet and fragrant almond cakes, warm from the oven.

Mr. Kang sits at the kitchen table and thinks about the sun showing through the trees in the park or the moon peeking into his window. He listens to words in his head, then he picks up his brush and paints a poem. Sometimes he paints a poem twice to practice his brushwork. Mrs. Kang hangs the poems on the kitchen cabinets.

And then, after making sure that the door and the windows are shut, Mr. Kang opens his hua mei's cage. Speaking softly, he invites the bird to stand on the table.

Mr. Kang cleans the cage with a damp towel and dries it with a soft cloth. He takes out the hand-painted ceramic water bowl, rinses it, and puts it back in its stand, full of cool, clear water. He washes the hand-painted ceramic food bowl and puts it back, full of his own special recipe of millet coated with egg yolks and mixed with chopped meat. These days this is the only cooking Mr. Kang does.

Last, Mr. Kang takes a small piece of silk cloth, dampens it with water not too hot, not too cold, and gently wipes the sleek gray feathers of his bird. The hua mei walks right back into his cage. He prefers to give himself a bath.

"Never mind, Birdie," says Mr. Kang. "Instead of the bath, I'll read you my poem. I know you can understand. We both left our homeland. We still speak the old language."

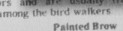

Rushing to the Golden Dragon
against a chilly wind,
the icy tears on my cheeks melt
with memories of warm old days.

Those who never left their home
stay safe, wrapped
in the arms of their motherfather land.
When they look out
their narrow windows,
they see their own kitchen gardens.
They know every plum tree, every kumquat,
every blade of grass, each gray pebble.

We, who long ago tossed on cold waters
looking only straight ahead
watch our city mountains
from wide windows, tall rooftops.
Yet our old hearts hold old places.
We save, in old, grown heads,
a full-blown rose in summer,
the sound of bamboo leaves when
the wind is gentle,
the taste of mooncakes.

The hua mei sings his own melody back
to Mr. Kang. Mr. Kang closes his eyes to listen.
"Beautiful, Birdie. You are a good poet
and a good friend to me," says Mr. Kang.

313

Sam usually comes to visit on Saturdays. If Mr. Kang is cleaning the cage, then the hua mei sings to Sam. Sam holds out his finger, and the hua mei holds on tightly. They stare at each other, each without blinking.

"Did he really fly from China?" Sam asks one time.

"In an airplane," says Mr. Kang. "China is so far, even for a bird."

"You should let him go. Maybe he wants to fly home."

"I don't think he could without an airplane. Anyway, he's like me. Home is here with you. If he went home now, I think he would miss his Sundays on Delancey Street." Mr. Kang puts his arm around Sam's shoulders and hugs him.

"I have a very smart grandson," he sighs. "Maybe one day we can visit China together."

And this is how Mr. Kang spends his days, except for Sundays.

On Sundays Mr. Kang gets up when it's dark. He washes his face and puts on his clothes. When he is ready, he picks up the cage by the ring on top. The freshly ironed cover is tied shut, and the bird is still sleeping. As he opens the door to leave the apartment, Mrs. Kang is padding quickly behind him.

"Wait for me!" she calls.

"Shhhh!" says Mr. Kang, but he waits as she closes the door and turns her key.

Mr. Kang and his bird lead the way. He walks gingerly, holding onto the banister to steady himself as he goes down the stairs. Out the door, down the block, across the street he glides, to Sara Delano Roosevelt Park on Delancey Street.

Mrs. Kang follows, three steps behind. She sees her friends and slips away to join them.

Mr. Kang hangs the cage on the fence, stretches his arms, and breathes in the morning.

Mr. Lum arrives with a cage in each hand. "How are you, my friend? How is the bird?"

"We are enjoying the morning," smiles Mr. Kang.

"Mr. Lum!
When I see your cages
resting on the green ivy floor
of Sara Delano Roosevelt Park in New York,

I remember my arm is lifted up to hold
Grandfather's big hand
and that ivy is green
from the Shanghai sun
and that ginkgo tree is blowing
in the soft Shanghai breeze
and that heat in my breast
is from my sweet and fragrant almond cake.
Grandmother slipped it into my pocket,
and it is still there,
warm from her oven."

"Even when you speak a greeting to your friend you are painting a poem," says Mr. Lum. Mr. Kang bows his head.

Today is a special Sunday morning because Sam and Mr. Kang are going to the park together. Sam slept at his grandparents' house last night. It is still dark, and he is rubbing his eyes as he jumps from his bed. Just like Grandpa, he washes his face and puts on his clothes. Together, at dawn's first light, they lift the cage. The cover is still tied, the bird is still sleeping. Sam opens the front door. Grandpa steps out, and Grandma is there right behind him, just as she is every Sunday morning.

"Wait for me!" she says.

"Shhhh!" say Mr. Kang and Sam, but they wait as she closes the door. Mrs. Kang takes one extra minute to slip two warm almond cakes into Sam's pocket. Then Sam and Mr. Kang lead the way down the stairs, out the front door, on to the corner, across the street, all the way to Sara Delano Roosevelt Park on Delancey Street.

As usual, Mrs. Kang follows until she sees her friends. Sam sets the bird cage gently on the ground. Mr. Lum's cages are already hanging.

"Look who's here!" says Mr. Lum. "How are you, Sam? You're getting so big. How old are you?"

"Seven," says Sam.

"Only seven?" says Mr. Lum. "You're handling that cage better than a twelve-year-old would!"

Sam smiles.

"An old grandfather does not mind growing old in a foreign land with such a grandson," says Mr. Kang.

"I am happy in this strange land:
I see my grandson planted
in the new, rich earth,
growing straight and smart and tall.
I water him.
The sun shines on his
firm young leaves
as I watch for his flowers
and for his fruit."

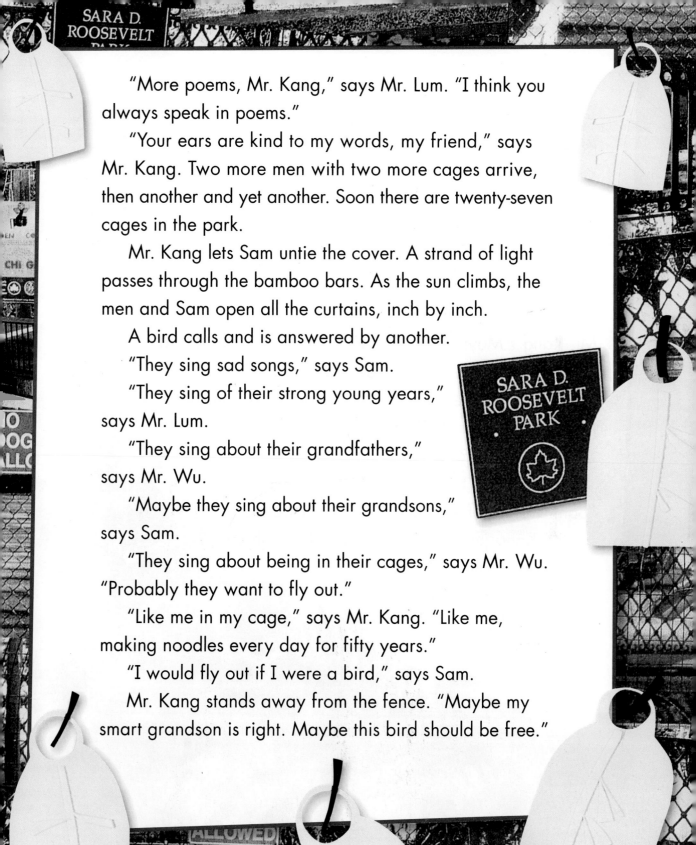

"More poems, Mr. Kang," says Mr. Lum. "I think you always speak in poems."

"Your ears are kind to my words, my friend," says Mr. Kang. Two more men with two more cages arrive, then another and yet another. Soon there are twenty-seven cages in the park.

Mr. Kang lets Sam untie the cover. A strand of light passes through the bamboo bars. As the sun climbs, the men and Sam open all the curtains, inch by inch.

A bird calls and is answered by another.

"They sing sad songs," says Sam.

"They sing of their strong young years," says Mr. Lum.

"They sing about their grandfathers," says Mr. Wu.

"Maybe they sing about their grandsons," says Sam.

"They sing about being in their cages," says Mr. Wu. "Probably they want to fly out."

"Like me in my cage," says Mr. Kang. "Like me, making noodles every day for fifty years."

"I would fly out if I were a bird," says Sam.

Mr. Kang stands away from the fence. "Maybe my smart grandson is right. Maybe this bird should be free."

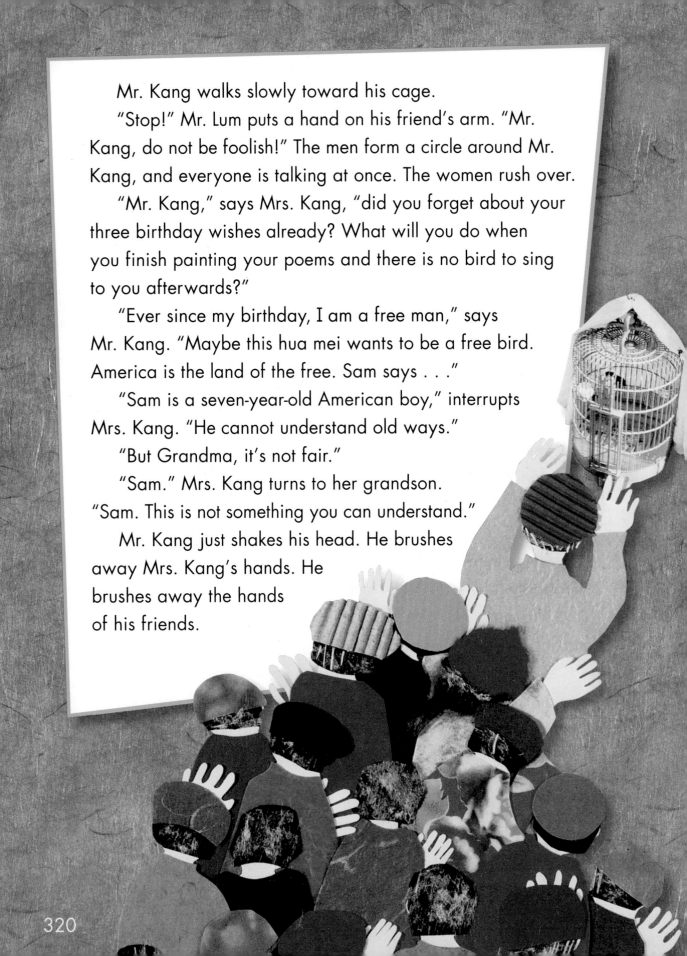

Mr. Kang walks slowly toward his cage.

"Stop!" Mr. Lum puts a hand on his friend's arm. "Mr. Kang, do not be foolish!" The men form a circle around Mr. Kang, and everyone is talking at once. The women rush over.

"Mr. Kang," says Mrs. Kang, "did you forget about your three birthday wishes already? What will you do when you finish painting your poems and there is no bird to sing to you afterwards?"

"Ever since my birthday, I am a free man," says Mr. Kang. "Maybe this hua mei wants to be a free bird. America is the land of the free. Sam says . . ."

"Sam is a seven-year-old American boy," interrupts Mrs. Kang. "He cannot understand old ways."

"But Grandma, it's not fair."

"Sam." Mrs. Kang turns to her grandson. "Sam. This is not something you can understand."

Mr. Kang just shakes his head. He brushes away Mrs. Kang's hands. He brushes away the hands of his friends.

Suddenly Sam is frightened. What if Grandma is right? What if Grandpa is sorry after the hua mei flies away? What if the hua mei gets lost? What if he starves? What if he dies?

"Grandpa, wait," says Sam. But Grandpa does not hear. Mr. Kang cannot hear any voice except the voice inside his own head, inside his own heart. He opens the bamboo door.

Mr. Kang's hua mei perches on the threshold of his cage. Perhaps he thinks it's cage-cleaning time. He slowly steps out. He stops to sing a long, sweet note, turns his head to the breeze, and flies into the sky.

Mr. Kang takes off his cap and covers his heart with his hand. For a moment there is silence. Mrs. Kang bends her head and hugs herself. Her mouth is a thin straight line. "Oh, Mr. Kang," she whispers in Chinese. "What can you be thinking?" Sam starts to cry.

"Sam and I are going home to paint poems," says Mr. Kang loudly, in English.

He lifts his empty cage, takes Sam's hand, and together they walk out of the park. Onto the sidewalk, over to the corner, across the street, up the block they walk.

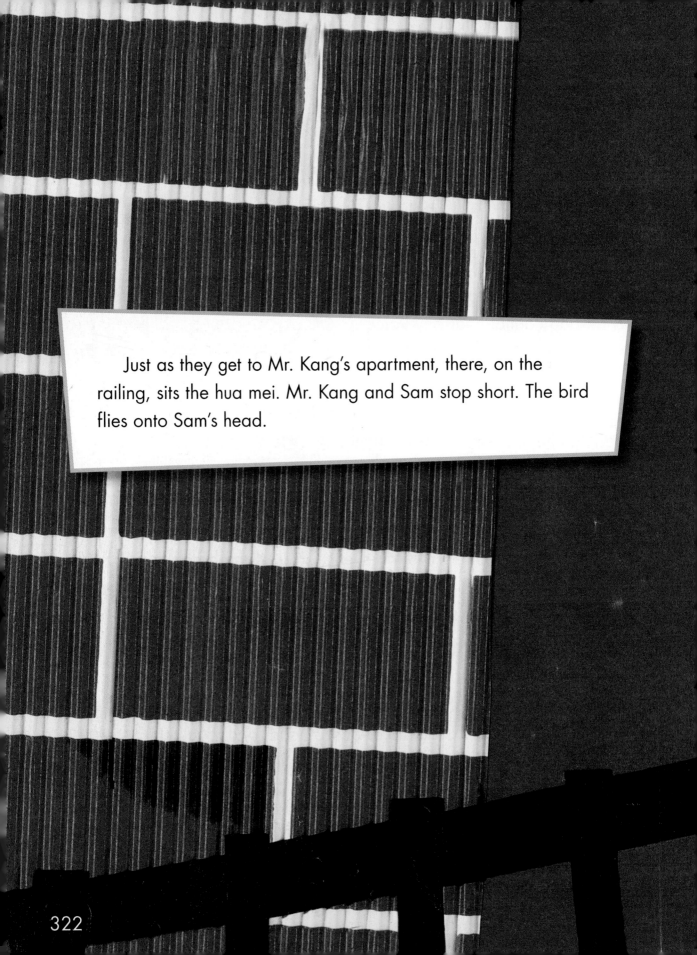

Just as they get to Mr. Kang's apartment, there, on the railing, sits the hua mei. Mr. Kang and Sam stop short. The bird flies onto Sam's head.

Then up the stairs and into the kitchen they run. They sit at the table, coats and caps still on. The hua mei hops onto Sam's paper. Mr. Kang paints his poem as Sam paints his picture. The bird helps.

After forty-three American years
I still speak my native tongue,
but any Chinese ear can hear
that I no longer speak
like a native. Sometimes

even I can hear
the familiar sounds bending
by themselves in my own throat,
coming out strangely,
sounding a little American. Yet

those same words in English suffer more.
I open up
my American mouth and
no one needs to see my face to know
my ship was never Mayflower. But

at home, with even you, my hua mei, peeping
a little like a sparrow,
I sit at my kitchen table, and I paint these words.
They sing out without accent:
We are Americans, by choice.

"This is your poem, Birdie," says Mr. Kang, "and Sam, it's your poem too."

Then Mr. Kang looks at Sam's painting. "My grandson is a great artist," he says. He hangs the paintings on the kitchen cabinet and sits back to admire them.

Mrs. Kang walks into the kitchen with her mouth still in that thin straight line, but there is the bird, and suddenly she is smiling.

"Today I'll cook for both of you, and for your hua mei," she says.

And she makes tea, and more sweet and fragrant almond cakes, warm from the oven.

Reader Response

Open for Discussion Read Mr. Kang's first poem out loud. Then read his last poem out loud. Why are the two poems so different from each other?

1. Find the most interesting illustration in the story. Pretend that you are the artist. Explain how and why you made that illustration. **Think Like an Author**

2. What caused Mr. Kang to change his mind about his *hua mei*? **Cause and Effect**

3. Did you create a graphic organizer as you read? If so, tell how it helped you. If not, what kind of graphic organizer could have helped? Tell why. **Graphic Organizer**

4. Write Mr. Kang a note to wish him a happy birthday. Use words from the Words to Know list and from the story. **Vocabulary**

Look Back and Write Sam told his grandfather to make a birthday wish. What did Mr. Kang wish? Look back at page 311. Write about the wish. Use details from the story in your answer.

Meet author **and illustrator Susan L. Roth on page 418.**

Write Now

Outline

Prompt

Happy Birthday Mr. Kang tells about a special bird and a wish.

Think about some of the facts in the story. Now use the story and the library or Internet to outline a topic from the story.

Student Model

Important details are shown with Roman numerals.

Information is organized into topics and subtopics.

Writer used complete <u>sentences</u> instead of phrases in this outline.

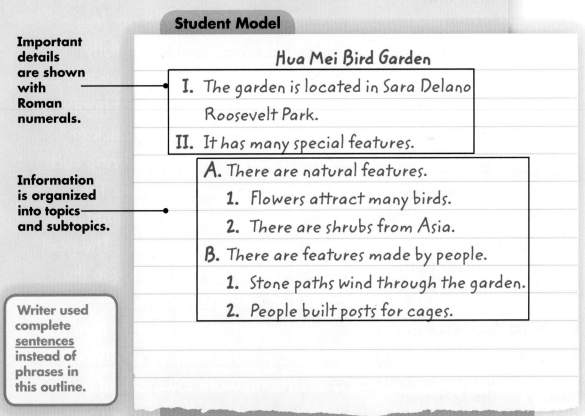

Hua Mei Bird Garden

I. The garden is located in Sara Delano Roosevelt Park.

II. It has many special features.

  A. There are natural features.

    1. Flowers attract many birds.

    2. There are shrubs from Asia.

  B. There are features made by people.

    1. Stone paths wind through the garden.

    2. People built posts for cages.

Use the model to help you write your own outline.

Interview

Genre

- In an interview, an expert shares his or her knowledge about a subject.

- An interview is written in a question-and-answer format.

Text Features

- The names of the interviewer and the expert answering the questions usually appear in dark print. The names are sometimes abbreviated.

- Photographs often help the reader better understand the subject.

Link to Science

Learn more about animal rescue programs. Use the library or the Internet. Create a brochure that will encourage people to use one program.

Back to the WILD

A Talk with a Wildlife Worker

by Melissa Blackwell Burke

Animals in the wild are free. They do what comes naturally to them. They don't have people taking care of them. What happens when a wild animal gets sick or hurt? Sometimes people bring such animals to a wildlife clinic. The clinic takes care of the animal until it can care for itself again. The goal is to get the animal back into the wild as soon as possible.

The staff at the Wildlife Medical Clinic at the University of Illinois in Urbana work toward that goal. We spoke to Molly Jean Carpenter, a volunteer at the clinic. She shared her thoughts about working with wildlife and described an amazing experience.

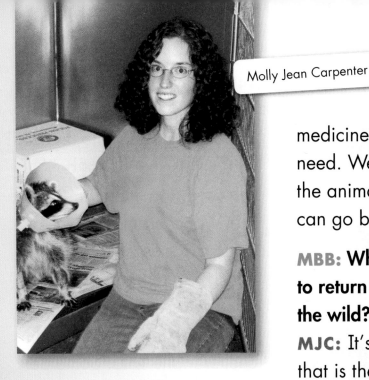

Molly Jean Carpenter

medicine and care that they need. We do our best to help the animal recover so that it can go back into the wild.

MBB: Why is it so important to return these animals to the wild?

MJC: It's important because that is their home! It is very stressful for a wild animal to lose its freedom. They need to do all the activities that are natural for them, such as running, hunting, or soaring.

MELISSA BLACKWELL BURKE: How do workers decide when an animal needs care in your clinic?

MOLLY JEAN CARPENTER: Concerned citizens rescue animals that have been hurt. Or sometimes they bring in a young animal that isn't being cared for by its kind. We examine the animal from its head to its tail. If the animal can't take care of itself in the wild, we admit it to our clinic. We feed the animals, clean them, and give them any

Wildlife rescue at work

 Cause and Effect What causes animals to be brought to the clinic?

329

Black-footed ferret being released into the wild

Pets depend on people.

MBB: If freedom is important for wildlife, should people release their pets into the wild?

MJC: Pets should not be released into the wild because many pets are not suited for a life outdoors. Pets could be hurt by wildlife or weather conditions. They may have a hard time finding food and shelter in the wild. Some pets might even hurt wildlife. It is much safer, for both pets and for wildlife, if pets stay with their owners.

MBB: Tell us about one of your favorite animal success stories at the clinic.

MJC: My favorite patient was a red-tailed hawk named Copernicus. Copernicus was hit by a car. He had a broken wing and a broken leg. He had surgery at the clinic to help his bones heal. We fed and cleaned Copernicus. We gave him treatments every day. He grew stronger and more aggressive. It was his way of

Red-tailed hawk in flight

telling us that he wanted to return to the wild. In a couple of months, Copernicus had shown us that he could take care of himself in the wild. We prepared for his release. We found a place with fields and trees where Copernicus could find food and shelter. We took him out of his carrier. He flew straight out into the sky and soared! Then he perched himself at the top of a tall tree. It was an incredible experience that I'll never forget!

REMEMBER: *Wild animals belong in the wild! If you come across a hurt animal, check your phone book for a clinic that helps wild animals and returns them to their homes.*

Reading Across Texts
How was Mr. Kang's *hua mei* different from Copernicus, the red-tailed hawk in this interview?

Writing Across Texts Write a paragraph explaining which bird you think was better off and why.

 **Graphic Organizers** Be sure to add information to your graphic organizer.

Fact and Opinion

- A statement of fact tells something that can be proved true or false. You can find proof by reading, observing, or asking an expert.

- A statement of opinion tells ideas or feelings about something.

- Words such as *great, best,* and *worst* can be clues to statements of opinion.

Statement	Fact or Opinion?

Strategy: Answer Questions

Good readers know where to look for answers to questions. Specific facts are particularly easy to locate. Sometimes the answer is right there in the text. Other times, you will have to combine what you already know with what is in the text. A fact in the text could be an answer to a question you are asked.

Write to Read

1. Read "Paint." Look for statements of fact and statements of opinion in the article.

2. Make a chart like the one above. Fill in your chart as you read the article.

Paint

Paint is one of the greatest things in the world. But what is it?

Paint has two main parts. The first is pigment, which is a powder that gives the paint its color. The other main part is a liquid, such as water. The liquid usually has something called a resin dissolved in it. To make paint, the pigment and the liquid are mixed together. After you paint a surface, the liquid part of the paint dries but the pigment stays on the surface. You should always buy the cheapest paint you can find.

People have been making and using paints for thousands of years. When people lived in caves, some of them used paints to make pictures on the walls. These paintings were a lot better than some of the modern art hanging in museums. Today, people still use paint to make pictures on walls. These pictures are called murals.

Skill Here is a statement of fact. How can you tell?

Strategy If you were asked the question "How long have people been making and using paints?" here's where you would find the answer—right there in the text.

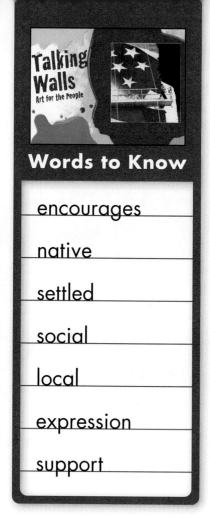

Words to Know

encourages

native

settled

social

local

expression

support

Vocabulary Strategy
for Unfamiliar Words

Glossary Sometimes you can use a glossary to find the meaning of an unknown word. A glossary is a list of important words in a book and their meanings. The words are listed in alphabetical order. The glossary is usually at the back of the book.

1. Turn to the glossary at the back of the book.

2. Use the first letters of the word to help you find it in the glossary.

3. Read the meaning of the word. Then try the meaning in the sentence. Does it make sense?

As you read "Class Art," use the glossary to find out the meanings of the vocabulary words.

Class Art

Ms. Ramsey's students are excited. They are planning to paint a mural on one wall in their classroom. Ms. Ramsey encourages the students to talk about what they will paint on the mural. Everyone has a different idea. Julio's family came to the United States from Mexico. He wants to paint something about his native country and his new country. Mary wants to paint something about the community's history. Her family settled here a long, long time ago. Gerrard thinks the mural should show the social life of the people who live in the community. Diana thinks the mural should be more about global, not local, issues. It should show how the community is part of the world. How can the students get all these ideas on one mural? Ms. Ramsey points out that the mural should be an expression of the group's interests and beliefs. She says that with a little planning, the students can paint a mural that will support everyone's ideas.

Words to Write

Imagine you and your classmates are going to paint a mural. Tell what you think the mural should show. Use words from the Words to Know list.

Talking Walls

Art for the People

by Katacha Díaz

What do these talking walls have to say?

Immigrants travel to America from all over the world. They leave behind homes and villages in their native countries for the promise of a better life and for the freedom this country has to offer.

The people in America enjoy many different kinds of freedom, including the freedom of artistic expression. Writers, musicians, dancers, and artists are free to speak their minds through their art — in any way they choose. Do you know that some painters use walls as their canvas? These painted walls are called murals and are often painted in public places for all the people of the community to see.

Muralists are asked by a town, school, or business to create a work of art on a wall. Muralists paint many different kinds of murals. Some are inside, some are outside. Some tell the history of a town and everyday life of the people who settled there. Others show special celebrations and community festivals. Still others depict symbols of American freedom and democracy at work. All are great examples of artistic expression at its best.

"Community of Music," Long Beach, California ▶

Immigrant

On the walls of a meat market in Los Angeles is a mural about immigrants painted by Hector Ponce. It tells the history of the people who live in the Pico and Hoover neighborhood. This mural, titled "Immigrant," shows the Statue of Liberty just beyond reach and Latin American immigrants working hard to provide for their families. Do you see a woman with young children, a man selling bags of oranges, a seamstress, and a man looking for cans to recycle?

Hector Ponce, the artist, came from El Salvador more than 15 years ago. He says, "My mural shows what's in the hearts of many people who come to this country looking for a better life."

▲ "Immigrant," Los Angeles, California ▶

Reach High and You Will Go Far

Before artist Joshua Sarantitis creates a mural, he talks with the people of the community. He listens to their stories about the neighborhood. He interprets their stories by making sketches, and then he makes plans for the painting of the mural.

Over the years, Sarantitis has created many public murals across America, including "Reach High and You Will Go Far." This mural honors the hopes and dreams of the many children who live in a downtown neighborhood in Philadelphia. The painting is beautiful. It shows a young girl with her arms held high. Her hands and fingers become a tree rising over the building. The artist fashioned the top of the tree as a billboard extending above the roof to show how people can grow and change. The mural encourages children to reach for the future through education.

"Reach High and You Will Go Far,"
Philadelphia, Pennsylvania ▶

A Shared Hope

Paul Botello was 8 years old when he began helping his older brother, David, paint murals. Paul loved painting murals and was inspired to become an artist like his brother. When Paul graduated from high school, he went on to college to study art. Today he creates and paints murals, and he teaches art too!

Paul painted a special mural called "A Shared Hope" for an elementary school in Los Angeles, California. Most of the students at Esperanza School are immigrants from Central America. The mural speaks to the schoolchildren. It tells them that education is the key to success.

At the top of the mural, a teacher helps guide her students over the building blocks of life. Students are standing at the bottom of the painting holding objects that symbolize their future. Their parents stand behind to help guide and support them. Teachers, students, and parents from the school posed for the artist and his assistants as they created the mural.

"Education, hope, and immigration are my themes," says Paul Botello. "People immigrate to the United States because they hope for a better life. Through education, a better life can be accomplished."

"A Shared Hope," Los Angeles, California

345

Dreams of Flight

David Botello—the older brother of Paul—loved to paint and dreamed of becoming an artist. When he was in the third grade, he and his art partner, Wayne Healy, painted a mural of a dinosaur in art class. Little did David know that that dinosaur mural was the first of many murals he would paint with Wayne.

Years later, the childhood friends, now both artists, decided to go into business together painting murals. David and Wayne often create and paint murals together, but not always.

David painted a large mural called "Dreams of Flight" at Estrada Courts, a public housing project in Los Angeles. He says, "I've always wanted this mural to speak to the children who see it, and to say, 'Your dreams can come true.'"

It's interesting to note that when the artist repainted the mural seventeen years after it was originally completed, he changed one of the children from a boy to a girl. Much had changed over the years, and the artist wanted all children to know that girls can dream of flying model airplanes too. It is the artist's hope that over time the mural will inspire many of the children who see it to work hard and follow their dreams.

"Dreams of Flight," Los Angeles, California

Talking Walls

Cities, large and small, invite artists to paint special murals in public places for everyone to see. Murals are talking walls; they speak to the people.

Community murals tell stories of personal, political, and social beliefs of the local residents. Some murals inspire or amuse us, while others stir our hearts.

"Declaration of Independence, 1776" was painted by Allyn Cox in the U.S. Capitol, Washington, D.C.

From sea to shining sea, the artists who create art for the people are instrumental in reminding Americans everywhere of the freedoms that help our democracy work.

Muralists use scaffolding to reach large murals.

The "American Flag" mural was painted by Meg Saligman in Philadelphia, Pennsylvania. ▼

Reader Response

Open for Discussion Look once more at the murals shown in this article. Now it is your turn. Describe an important mural you would plan and paint.

1. An author can help you look at art. Read sentences by Katacha Díaz that help you understand and enjoy the art in this article. **Think Like an Author**

2. This selection is full of facts. What could you do to prove that these are true facts? Now look on page 338. What clue word signals an opinion on this page? **Fact and Opinion**

3. This selection tells about two brothers who are both muralists. Who are they and where do they live? Is the answer in the book or in your head? **Answer Questions**

4. Explain this statement: Murals are a public form of artistic expression. Use words from the Words to Know list and from the selection. **Vocabulary**

Look Back and Write Why did David Botello change his mural after 17 years? Look back at page 347. Use information from the selection to support your answer.

Meet author **Katacha Diaz on page 416.**

Write Now

Informational Paragraph

Prompt

Talking Walls describes special murals. Think about a kind of art that you know well. Now write an informational paragraph about this kind of art.

Writing Trait

Organize your writing by arrranging your ideas in a **paragraph.**

Paragraph begins with sentence that grabs readers' attention.

Student Model

Clay can't move by itself, but a special kind of art can make clay look like it's moving. Clay animation begins with a story. Then an artist draws pictures like a cartoon and uses the pictures to make characters out of clay. Next, the artist films the characters. After moving the characters a tiny bit each time, the artist takes a picture. Later, when you watch the film, the clay characters look like they're moving. This kind of art takes a long time to make, but it's fun to watch clay come to life!

Sequence words help <u>organize</u> steps in process.

Last sentence returns to topic of art mentioned in opening sentence.

Use the model to help you write your own informational paragraph.

Poetry

Genre

- Poetry can be a way to express feelings.

- Poems are a mixture of words with rhythm, which may or may not rhyme.

Text Features

- This poem is written in the first person.

- There is very little punctuation in this poem. Why do you think the writer chose this approach?

Link to Reading

With a partner, search the library for a poem or rap that you enjoy. Together, recite your choice to the class.

Nathaniel's Rap

by Eloise Greenfield

It's Nathaniel talking
and Nathaniel's me
I'm talking about
my philosophy
About the things I do
And the people I see
All told in the words
Of Nathaniel B. Free
That's me
And I can rap
I can rap
I can
rap,
rap,
rap
Till your earflaps flap

I can talk that talk
Till you go for a walk
I can run it on down
Till you get out of town

I can rap
I can rap

Rested, dressed and feeling fine
I've got something on my mind
Friends and kin and neighborhood
Listen now and listen good
Nathaniel's talking
Nathaniel B. Free
Talking about
My philosophy

Been thinking all day
I got a lot to say
Gotta run it on down
Nathaniel's way
Okay!
I gotta rap
Gotta rap
Gotta rap, rap, rap
Till your earflaps flap
Gotta talk that talk
Till you go for a walk
Gotta run it on down
Till you get out of town

Gotta rap
Gotta rap

Rested, dressed and feeling fine
I've got something on my mind
Friends and kin and neighborhood
Listen now and listen good

I'm gonna rap, hey!
Gonna rap, hey!
Gonna rap, hey!
I'm gonna rap!

Reading Across Texts

The selection about murals and this rap poem tell of different forms of expression. What is one message you learned from each selection?

Writing Across Texts

Write the message that means the most to you and tell why.

 Rhythm   Snap your fingers or tap your toes as you read. Does it help?

Comprehension

Skill
Plot and Theme

Strategy
Visualize

 **Plot and Theme**

- The important events in a story make up the plot.

- The plot has a beginning, a middle, and an end.

- The "big idea" of the story is called the theme.

- The theme can be stated in a single sentence.

(**Beginning**) → (**Middle**) → (**End**)

Strategy: Visualize

Good readers use their imaginations to picture what is happening at the beginning, the middle, and the end of a story. As you read, pretend you are watching a movie of the story inside your head! This will help you keep track of the plot.

Write to Read

1. Read "The Ant and the Beetle." Make a graphic organizer like the one above to show the plot of the story.

2. Write the theme—or moral— of the story, using just one sentence.

The Ant and the Beetle

Adapted from Aesop's "The Fox and the Crow"

Annie Ant was famished. She stole a piece of cheese from an abandoned picnic and scrambled up to sit on a rock. She was about to eat the cheese when she noticed a beetle nearby.

The beetle had been spying on her, and having grown tired of his dull menu of leaves, he wanted the cheese for himself. He made a plan.

"My, my, I have never seen such a beautiful ant. From the tip of your antennae to the end of your abdomen, you are simply gorgeous!" flattered the beetle.

Annie thought, "Finally, someone who appreciates my true beauty."

"It is a shame," said the beetle. "Such a beauty must be delicate. Surely, you are not strong enough to help the other ants."

Now Annie Ant was insulted. How dare he suggest she was weak. "Hmph! I can lift this rock that is twice my size," she said.

Annie Ant set down the cheese and lifted the rock over her head.

The beetle grabbed the cheese and began to scurry away. "Yes, you are very strong, but you are also very foolish."

Strategy Here is a good place to visualize. What picture do you have in your mind of Annie Ant?

Skill In a fable, the theme is usually a lesson to be learned. It is called the *moral*. What lesson did the ant learn at the end of this story?

Words to Know

goal

discovery

scoop

crystal

journey

joyful

disappeared

unaware

Remember

Try the strategy. Then, if you need more help, use your glossary or a dictionary.

Vocabulary Strategy
for Prefixes and Suffixes

Word Structure When you see a word you don't know, look closely at the word. Does it have a prefix or suffix? The prefixes *un-* or *dis-* at the beginning of a word make the word mean "not ___" or "the opposite of ___." For example, *unhappy* means "not happy," and *disagree* means "the opposite of agree." The suffix *-ful* at the end of a word makes a word mean "full of." For example, *joyful* means "full of joy." You can use *un-, dis-,* or *-ful* to help you figure out the meaning of a word you don't know.

1. Put your finger over the prefix or suffix.

2. Look at the base word. Put the base word in the appropriate phrase:
"not___" for *un-*
"the opposite of ___" for *dis-*
"full of ___" for *-ful*

3. Try that meaning in the sentence. Does it make sense?

Read "How Ants Find Food." Look for words that have a prefix or suffix. Use the prefix or suffix to help you figure out the meanings of the words.

How Ants Find Food

Ants are social insects. Like wasps and bees, they live in large groups called colonies. The queen ant lays all the eggs, and the worker ants build the nest, look for food, care for the eggs, and defend the nest.

Ants that look for food are called scouts. Their goal is to find food and report the locations to the ants back at the nest. Suppose a scout ant makes this discovery: Someone has left out a scoop of sugar. The scout carries a sugar crystal back to the nest. On its return journey, the scout ant also leaves a scent trail leading from the food to the nest. When the other ants realize that the scout has found food, they become very excited. They seem joyful about the news. Many ants follow the scout's trail back to the food. They swarm over the sugar, picking up all the crystals. In a short time, all of the sugar has disappeared, and so have the ants. It happens so quickly that often people are unaware that ants were ever there at all.

Words to Write

Write about the jobs you think a worker ant does. Use words from the Words to Know list.

Two Bad Ants

by Chris Van Allsburg

Genre

An **animal fantasy** is a story with animal characters that behave like humans. What is unusual about these ants?

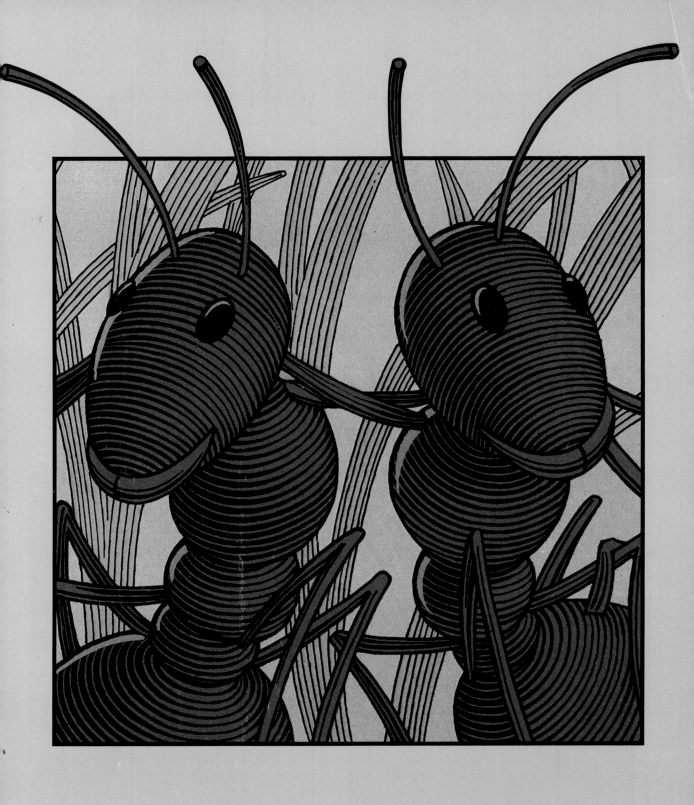

Who are these two bad ants,
and what do they do?

The news traveled swiftly through the tunnels of the ant world. A scout had returned with a remarkable discovery—a beautiful sparkling crystal. When the scout presented the crystal to the ant queen, she took a small bite, then quickly ate the entire thing.

She deemed it the most delicious food she had ever tasted. Nothing could make her happier than to have more, much more. The ants understood. They were eager to gather more crystals because the queen was the mother of them all. Her happiness made the whole ant nest a happy place.

It was late in the day when they departed. Long shadows stretched over the entrance to the ant kingdom. One by one the insects climbed out, following the scout, who had made it clear—there were many crystals where the first had been found, but the journey was long and dangerous.

They marched into the woods that surrounded their underground home. Dusk turned to twilight, twilight to night. The path they followed twisted and turned, every bend leading them deeper into the dark forest.

More than once the line of ants stopped and
anxiously listened for the sounds of hungry spiders.
But all they heard was the call of crickets echoing
through the woods like distant thunder.

Dew formed on the leaves above. Without
warning, huge cold drops fell on the marching ants.
A firefly passed overhead that, for an instant, lit up
the woods with a blinding flash of blue-green light.

At the edge of the forest stood a mountain. The ants looked up and could not see its peak. It seemed to reach right to the heavens. But they did not stop. Up the side they climbed, higher and higher.

The wind whistled through the cracks of the mountain's face. The ants could feel its force bending their delicate antennae. Their legs grew weak as they struggled upward. At last they reached a ledge and crawled through a narrow tunnel.

When the ants came out of the tunnel they found themselves in a strange world. Smells they had known all their lives, smells of dirt and grass and rotting plants, had vanished. There was no more wind and, most puzzling of all, it seemed that the sky was gone.

They crossed smooth shiny surfaces, then followed the scout up a glassy, curved wall. They had reached their goal. From the top of the wall they looked below to a sea of crystals. One by one the ants climbed down into the sparkling treasure.

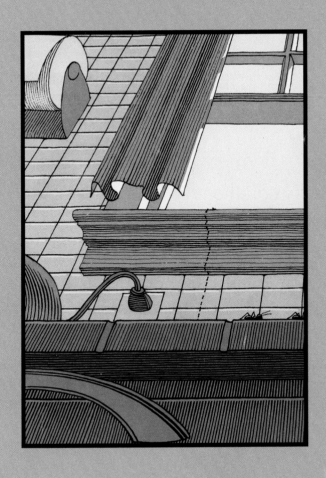

Quickly they each chose a crystal, then turned to start the journey home. There was something about this unnatural place that made the ants nervous. In fact they left in such a hurry that none of them noticed the two small ants who stayed behind.

"Why go back?" one asked the other. "This place may not feel like home, but look at all these crystals."

"You're right," said the other. "We can stay here and eat this tasty treasure every day, forever." So the two ants ate crystal after crystal until they were too full to move, and fell asleep.

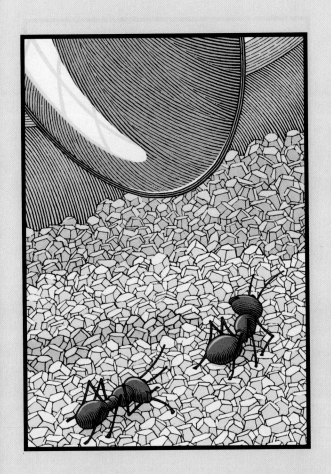

Daylight came. The sleeping ants were unaware of changes taking place in their new-found home. A giant silver scoop hovered above them, then plunged deep into the crystals. It shoveled up both ants and crystals and carried them high into the air.

The ants were wide awake when the scoop turned, dropping them from a frightening height. They tumbled through space in a shower of crystals and fell into a boiling brown lake.

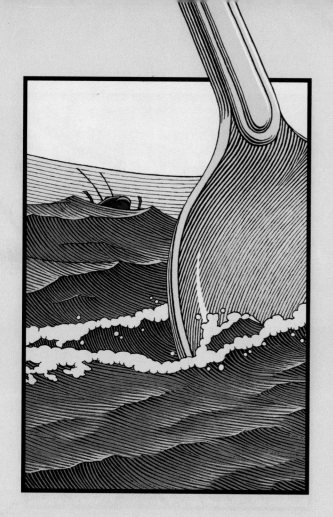 

Then the giant scoop stirred violently back and forth. Crushing waves fell over the ants. They paddled hard to keep their tiny heads above water. But the scoop kept spinning the hot brown liquid.

Around and around it went, creating a whirlpool that sucked the ants deeper and deeper. They both held their breath and finally bobbed to the surface, gasping for air and spitting mouthfuls of the terrible, bitter water.

Then the lake tilted and began to empty into a cave. The ants could hear the rushing water and felt themselves pulled toward the pitch-black hole. Suddenly the cave disappeared and the lake became calm. The ants swam to the shore and found that the lake had steep sides.

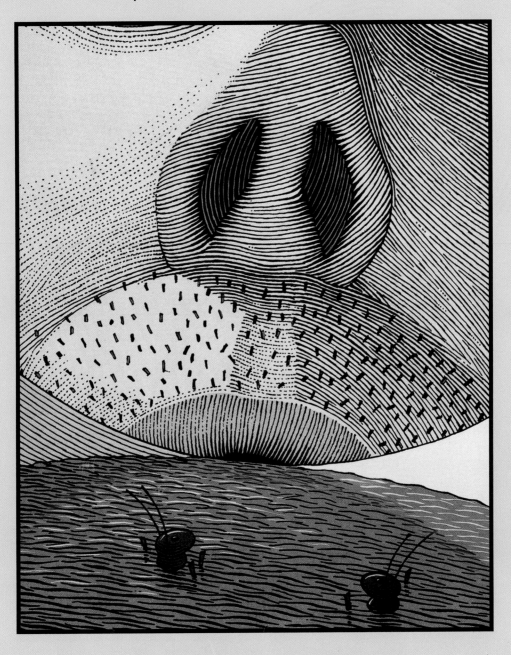

They hurried down the walls that held back the lake. The frightened insects looked for a place to hide, worried that the giant scoop might shovel them up again. Close by they found a huge round disk with holes that could neatly hide them.

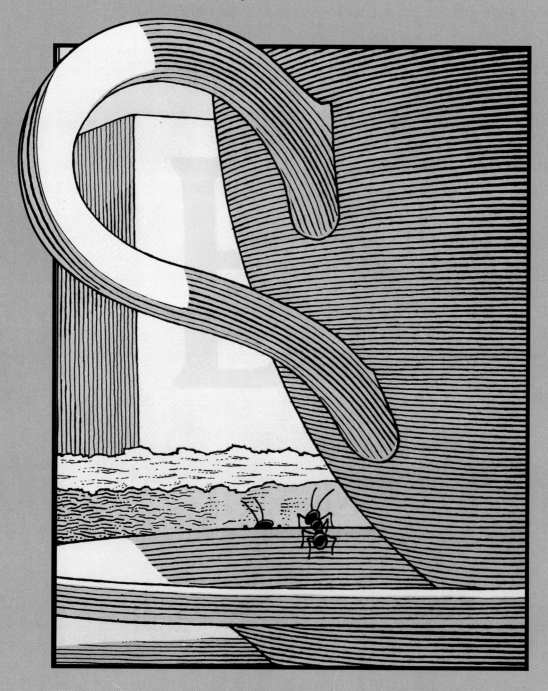

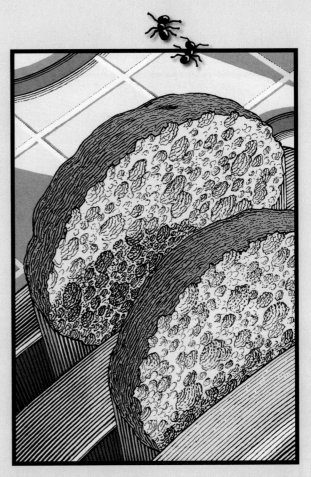

But as soon as they had climbed inside, their hiding place was lifted, tilted, and lowered into a dark space. When the ants climbed out of the holes, they were surrounded by a strange red glow. It seemed to them that every second the temperature was rising.

It soon became so unbearably hot that they thought they would soon be cooked. But suddenly the disk they were standing on rocketed upward, and the two hot ants went flying through the air.

They landed near what seemed to be a fountain—a waterfall pouring from a silver tube. Both ants had a powerful thirst and longed to dip their feverish heads into the refreshing water. They quickly climbed along the tube.

As they got closer to the rushing water the ants felt a cool spray. They tightly gripped the shiny surface of the fountain and slowly leaned their heads into the falling stream. But the force of the water was much too strong.

The tiny insects were pulled off the fountain and plunged down into a wet, dark chamber. They landed on half-eaten fruit and other soggy things. Suddenly the air was filled with loud, frightening sounds. The chamber began to spin.

The ants were caught in a whirling storm of shredded food and stinging rain. Then, just as quickly as it had started, the noise and spinning stopped. Bruised and dizzy, the ants climbed out of the chamber.

In daylight once again, they raced through puddles and up a smooth metal wall. In the distance they saw something comforting—two long, narrow holes that reminded them of the warmth and safety of their old underground home. They climbed up into the dark openings.

But there was no safety inside these holes. A strange force passed through the wet ants. They were stunned senseless and blown out of the holes like bullets from a gun. When they landed, the tiny insects were too exhausted to go on. They crawled into a dark corner and fell fast asleep.

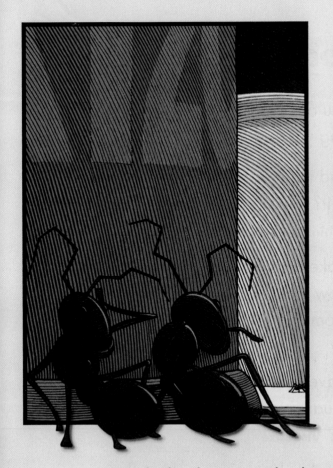

Night had returned when the battered ants awoke
to a familiar sound—the footsteps of their fellow insects
returning for more crystals. The two ants slipped quietly to
the end of the line. They climbed the glassy wall and once
again stood amid the treasure. But this time they each
chose a single crystal and followed their friends home.

Standing at the edge of their ant hole, the two ants
listened to the joyful sounds that came from below. They
knew how grateful their mother queen would be when
they gave her their crystals. At that moment, the two ants
felt happier than they'd ever felt before. This was their
home, this was their family. This was where they were
meant to be.

Reader Response

Open for Discussion You are a scientist tracking these two bad ants. Tell everything you see them do in this story.

1. How does the author and illustrator make you see the world the way ants see it? Read parts of the story to show what you mean. **Think Like an Author**

2. The decision the ants make leads to a huge problem for them. What is it, and how is it resolved? What do you think the ants learned from their experience? **Plot and Theme**

3. What picture did you have in your mind as you read page 373? How did visualizing help you understand what you were reading? **Visualize**

4. What might the two bad ants have to say about their adventure? Write a journal entry. Use words from the Words to Know list. **Vocabulary**

Look Back and Write Look back at pages 367–369 to find "a boiling brown lake," "a giant scoop," and "a cave." Write a note to tell the ants what these things really are.

Meet author and illustrator
Chris Van Allsburg on page 421.

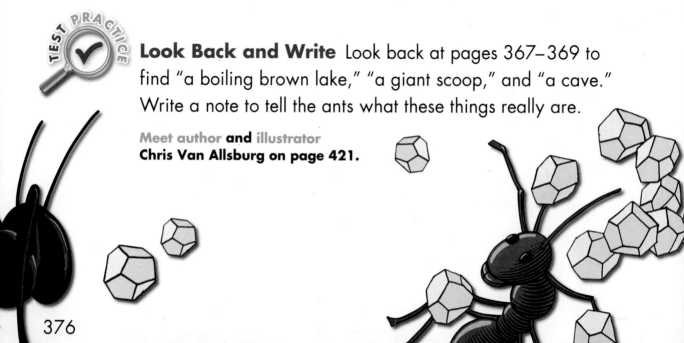

Writing About a Picture

Prompt

Two Bad Ants describes the adventures of two ants.

Think about a picture in the story you find interesting.

Now write about that picture, using vivid words.

Student Model

> To an ant, a small cup of coffee could seem like an enormous lake. A picture in Two Bad Ants shows ants, a cup of coffee, and the person drinking the coffee. Two ants are floating in a wavy pool of coffee. The cup is tipped toward another giant thing, the person's mouth. Huge lips are slurping coffee. What is that large prickly thing? It must be a mustache! Two long, shadowy holes are the person's nostrils. Notice that an ant's point of view is very different from ours.

Picture being described is identified.

Word choice includes exact nouns, strong verbs, and vivid adjectives.

Different kinds and lengths of sentences add variety to description.

Use the model to help you write about a picture.

377

Hiking Safety Tips

Evaluating Sources

Genre

- The Internet has a lot of information, but not all sources can be trusted.

- You need to learn how to tell which information is good and which is not.

Text Features

- Information following a link can help you decide whether a Web site might be useful.

- Web addresses ending in .gov or .org are usually good. Ask for help if you are not sure about a site.

Link to Social Studies

Search through newspapers and magazines for travel articles. Share what you learn with the class.

You are going on a camping trip. With camping comes freedom, but also dangers. You must prepare a list of hiking safety tips. You decide to use the Internet to help you.

For more practice

Take It to the Net

PearsonSuccessNet.com

You type the keyword "hiking" into an Internet search engine. The first two sites probably won't help. But the third site looks promising, so you click on Staying Safe on the Trail.

File   Edit

http://www.url.here

Search Engine

hiking   Search

<u>Hiking Clothes.</u> Outfit your family with these cute hiking shirts . . .

<u>Footwear.</u> We have 100% leather hiking boots, just what you're looking for . . .

<u>Staying Safe on the Trail.</u> Hiking is fun but beware of plants that . . .

File   Edit   View   Favorites   Tools   Help

http://

The list goes on. You print it out. Now you can enjoy the freedom of hiking in safety.

STAYING SAFE

A few tips will help you enjoy the freedom of a family hike in safety.

Drinking Water Don't hike anywhere without it, especially on hot days. Even the clearest stream water may not be safe.

Snacks Bring them to eat when you take breaks. Good hiking snacks include granola bars, trail mix, and crackers.

Poison Plants Beware of poison ivy and poison oak. Oil from the leaves can make you break out in a rash and blisters.

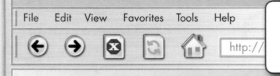

poison oak

Reading Across Texts

Which of these hiking tips could have helped the two bad ants?

Writing Across Texts Write a letter to the ants giving them these tips.

✓ Visualize   Try to visualize some of these dangers on the trail.

Generalize

- When you read, you may be given ideas about things or people. Sometimes, you can make a general statement about all of them together.

- This statement might tell how the things or people are all alike in some way.

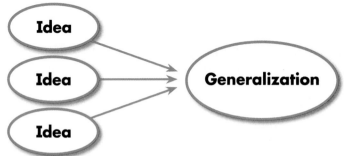

Strategy: Predict

Good readers think about what will come next as they read. Ask yourself: What has the author said about the topic so far? What else might I find out about? Try to take the ideas you've already read and make a generalization about or predict what will come next.

Write to Read

1. Read "Glassblowing." Look for ideas that tell how several things or people are all alike in some way.

2. Make a graphic organizer like the one above. Fill in your graphic organizer as you read the article.

Glassblowing

Syrian glassworkers invented the art of glassblowing more than 2,000 years ago. This method of shaping glass has changed very little since that time. The glassblower uses a hollow metal pipe that is about five feet long. On one end of the pipe is a mouthpiece. On the other end is a gob of hot melted glass. The worker blows air into the pipe, which causes the glass to expand into a hollow bubble. The worker then shapes the glass bubble into a container of some kind.

Strategy Here is a good place to predict. What do you think you will find out about next?

Sometimes the glassblower shapes the glass using a mold, as the ancient Syrians often did. But the basic process is the same. After blowing the glass into a bubble, the worker guides the bubble into a mold. Then, the worker blows through the pipe again until the glass bubble takes on the shape of the mold.

Today, glassblowing is often done by machines instead of people. But the basic process has stayed the same. All glassblowing requires melted glass and blowing air.

Skill The word *all* is a clue to a generalization. What generalization can you make about glassblowing?

Words to Know

glassblower

bursts

puffs

factory

burro

tune

reply

Remember

Try the strategy. Then, if you need more help, use your glossary or a dictionary.

Vocabulary Strategy
for Synonyms

Context Clues Sometimes when you are reading, you will see a word you don't know. The words nearby may help you figure out its meaning. Perhaps you will see a synonym for the word. A synonym is a word that has the same or almost the same meaning as another word. Look for a word you know that might be a synonym. See if it will help you understand the meaning of the word you don't know.

1. Look at the words around the word you don't know. Can you use them to figure out the meaning?

2. Perhaps the author used a synonym. Look for a word you know that might be a synonym, and use it to figure out the meaning of the unfamiliar word.

3. Try the synonym in place of the word in the sentence. Does it make sense?

As you read "At the Glassblower's," look for synonyms to help you understand the meanings of the vocabulary words.

At the GLASSBLOWER'S

You and some friends are watching a glassblower make beautiful glass pieces. The glassblower explains what she does. First she mixes sand, soda ash, and limestone together and heats them until they become liquid. Then she takes a hollow iron pipe about 5 feet long and dips one end into the liquid glass. She blows gently into the other end of the pipe, and a hollow glass bulge suddenly bursts out. She puffs again if she wants to make the bulge bigger. She twirls, stretches, and cuts the glass while it is soft. Then she removes the glass from the pipe and sets it aside to cool.

In a glass factory, the blowing might be done using molds and machines, but in this shop it is all done by hand. Here, you see glass vases, glass ornaments, and glass animals. A tiny glass burro, or donkey, even has a tiny saddle. Sets of glass chimes dangling from the ceiling play a tune when the wind blows. Their song sounds like tinkling bells. Everything shines and sparkles in the sunlight.

Your friends ask what you like best, and you reply, "I like when a new shape appears at the end of the pipe. What an amazing craft!"

Your friends smile and answer, "We think so too."

Words to Write

Write about a special glass object that you own or have seen. Describe it. Use words from the Words to Know list.

Elena's

Genre

Fantasy is a made-up story that could never happen. What makes this story a fantasy?

Serenade

by Campbell Geeslin   illustrated by Ana Juan

What happens when
Elena plays her serenade?

In Mexico the sun is called *el sol*, and the moon is called *la luna*. I am called Elena.

My papa is a glassblower. He puffs out his cheeks, blows into a long pipe, and a bottle appears at the other end, just like magic.

One afternoon I find an old pipe of Papa's. I ask him if he will teach me to be a glassblower too, but he shakes his head. "You are too little, Elenita, and the hot glass might burn you. Besides, who ever heard of a girl glassblower?"

Even though I am mad as a wet hen, I don't let Papa see my tears.

When I get home, my brother Pedro asks, "Why the sad face, Elena?"

"I want to blow glass, but Papa says I'm too little and anyway, who ever heard of a girl glassblower?"

"Monterrey is where the great glassblowers are," Pedro says. "You should go there."

Should I? I'm scared to leave Papa, but maybe I *should.*

The next morning I borrow a pair of Pedro's trousers, hide my hair under his old *sombrero,* and set out. Since girls aren't supposed to be glassblowers, I'll pretend that I am a boy.

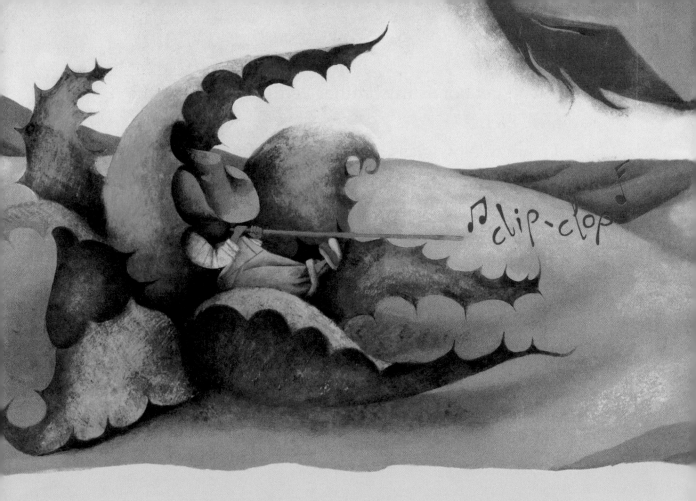

El sol blazes like Papa's furnace, and the road is long. I get hotter and hotter until, at last, I must rest. To pass the time, I puff out my cheeks and blow on my pipe. What is that? A pretty sound comes out!

Ever so gently I blow again. The notes get higher, *pree-tat-tat, pree-tat-tat.* I can hardly believe my ears— my pipe is making music!

I blow, easy and then harder, *pree-tat-tat,* until I find all the notes for a happy song called "Burro Serenade." I make the music go *clip-clop, clip-clop,* just the way a burro trots along.

Over and over I play the tune, my heart flying higher with every note. At last there are no mistakes.

♪ ♪ clip-clop ♪♪ clip-clop ♪

From behind a cactus Burro trots up and says, "Oh, *señor*, I was lost and lonely until I heard my song. Now I am smiling, see? May I take you someplace?"

"*Sí*," I say. "I am on my way to Monterrey to learn to be a glassblower."

"If you can make music, I'm sure you can make glass," Burro says. I climb on his back, and off we go.

It is almost evening when we overtake Roadrunner, limping along. "Oh, *Señor* Roadrunner," I say, "you are supposed to fly like the wind. *Qué pasa?*"

Roadrunner sighs. "I might as well be a turtle. Every time I try to run, one of my legs forgets how. Even a rock can go faster."

"Let's try this," I say. "I will blow my pipe slowly, and you step along with the music." I wonder if the steady beat of *"La Marcha Grande de Mejico"* will help. I sound out the notes until I have it just right.

Roadrunner's limp changes to a march. "Oh, that music makes me proud to be a Mexican!" he exclaims.

TUM, tum, TUM, tum. I play faster like a drum. *TUMtumTUMtumTUMtum.*

Suddenly, Roadrunner surges ahead. "Where are you going?" he calls back to me.

"I am on my way to Monterrey to learn to be a glassblower!" I shout.

"You play such a fine march, certainly you'll make a fine glassblower." His voice fades away as he disappears in a cloud of dust.

That evening, after *la luna grande* has risen, Burro lies down and I use him as a pillow. We have traveled all day, and we are tired. As I drift off to sleep, I think of home.

Sometime during the night I am awakened by awful howling. *La luna grande* is high in the sky and the desert is golden. Coyote runs toward us, chased by an owl, two bats, and a lizard who are hurling rocks at him.

"*Qué pasa, Señor* Coyote?" I ask.

His tongue hangs out and he puffs and puffs. "When *la luna* is bright, I sing—I can't help myself. But everyone hates my song."

"Let me hear you," I say.

Coyote throws back his head. "*Ouchowahooooo!*" he howls.

"Ay yah!" I cry.

The owl hoots, the bats shriek, and the lizard covers his ears.

"Listen to this," I say, "and sing along." I take my pipe and blow, very softly, a low note. It is the beginning of a song my papa used to sing to me, *"Cielito Lindo."*

"Hmmm, that sounds sweet as honey," Coyote says. "Let me try." He clears his throat and begins, "For when our hearts sing together, *ci-e-li-to lin-do,* love comes along . . ." His voice is soft and low.

"Bravo!" I shout.

"Bravo!" cry the owl, the bats, and the lizard.

The happy Coyote asks me where I am going. "I am on my way to Monterrey to become a glassblower."

"If you could teach me to sing, you can do anything!" he declares.

Then, as Coyote sings his sweet love song to *la luna,* Burro and I slip back into sleep.

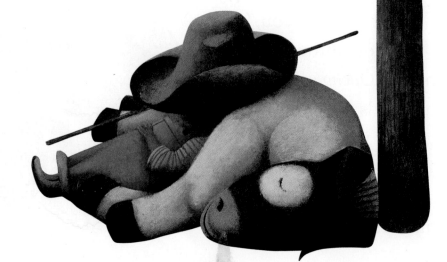

Next morning, Burro and I start off with the sunrise, and at last we get to Monterrey. There are many houses and buildings, and everyone is in a hurry. Before me is a factory where the furnace's giant mouth is full of bubbling glass.

"*Adiós, mi amigo,*" I say to Burro and then step inside.

In front of me, four big men stand stiff as soldiers, puffing on long pipes. As their balloon cheeks shrink, glass bubbles appear and turn into tall bottles, medium bottles, and tiny bottles.

"What do you want?" their boss yells at me.

I cough and in a low voice I say, *"Por favor, Señor . . .* I want to be a glassblower."

The men laugh. The boss winks and says, "Okay, *muchacho.* Let's see what you can do."

I twirl the end of my pipe in the hot glass just the way Papa does.

What is going to happen?

I close my eyes and gulp a deep breath. I puff out my cheeks and begin to play a song called *"Estrellita,"* about a little star.

When the men hear music, they laugh even harder. I think they will never stop, but then . . .

I remember how my pipe helped Burro, how it helped Roadrunner and Coyote.
I blow, strong and steady, and when I open my eyes, I have made a star!

The men's mouths drop open in surprise.

I tap the star off into the sand to cool, and then I play *"Estrellita"* again. At the end of my pipe another glass star bursts out.

The men try to blow music too, but only burping noises and crooked bottles come from their pipes.

"Welcome, little glassblower!" the boss says, and shakes my hand. He puts my stars in the factory windows where they twinkle like real stars.

As soon as the children in Monterrey see them, they all want one. The stars sell faster than I can blow them.

One night, when I am working alone, I get tired of playing *"Estrellita."* I twirl a huge glass glob onto the end of my pipe and begin a song called *"La Golondrina."* It is about a swallow gliding over the sea.

A glass bird appears. As I play, its wings grow long. I play on, and it becomes the size of Roadrunner. I take a quick breath to play more, and the glass bird grows as big as Coyote. I blow and blow, and my swallow becomes bigger than Burro.

I tap the bird off and the glass cools. The swallow's great wings stretch from one wall to the other.

Oh, I wish Papa could see what I can do!

After sliding open the factory's big back door, I push my bird out into the alley. I climb on and play *"La Golondrina"* again. Slowly the swallow rises into the air.

I'm flying! Down below, the lights shine from hundreds of windows with glass stars in them.

As I play my pipe the bird flies higher. I turn south, and when I see my town below, I play softer and softer and finally stop. The bird glides down onto a field of lilies. I run home, climb in the window, and curl up in my own little bed.

The next morning, when Papa goes off to work, I get up. I have a plan all figured out. I put on Pedro's pants and *sombrero* again, and then I tear a *tortilla* in half and paste it onto my chin with flour and water.

I take my pipe and run straight to Papa's factory.

"*Buenos días, señor*," I say, in an old man's shaky voice. "I am a glassblower, come all the way from Monterrey."

"Why, grandfather," Papa says politely, "you aren't as tall as your pipe. How can you blow glass?"

I twirl hot glass onto the end and begin to play a
song called *"La Mariposa,"* about how pretty butterflies
are. A glass butterfly floats from my pipe and flutters
about, its wings chiming.

"Qué bonita!" Papa exclaims. "If only my daughter
were here to see this."

"But she is!" I shout, and rip off my *tortilla* beard
and toss the *sombrero* in the air.

"Is that you, Elena?" Papa asks, squinting.

"At your service, Papa," I reply and laugh. Then I
tell him about all the funny and amazing things that
happened on my trip to Monterrey.

Now every day Papa and I work side by side at our great furnace. Papa blows bottles and pitchers and drinking glasses. I blow birds, stars, butterflies, and songs.

On Saturdays tourists come from all over to dance to the music and to try to catch a glass butterfly. If you close your eyes and sit absolutely still, you may hear their wings chiming like little glass bells. Listen. . . .

Reader Response

Open for Discussion Which parts of *Elena's Serenade* might be hard to believe? Suppose you asked Burro, Roadrunner, and Coyote about these parts. What would they say?

1. Some authors seem to have fun writing their stories. Read parts of *Elena's Serenade* that seem to show that the author had fun. **Think Like an Author**

2. What did you learn about Elena? How might she act in other situations? **Generalize**

3. What did you predict would happen when Elena met Roadrunner? Did you change your prediction as you read? If so, why? **Predict**

4. If prizes were given to unusual glassblowers, do you think Elena would get one? Make a list of reasons why she should—or should not. Use words from the Words to Know list. **Vocabulary**

Look Back and Write Elena pretends that she is an old man. Does Papa believe her? Look back at pages 398–399. Tell why you think as you do.

Meet author **Campbell Geeslin on page 421** and illustrator **Ana Juan on page 423.**

Write Now

Paragraph

Prompt

Elena's Serenade describes a girl who makes special music.

Think about a character or person you know well.

Now write a paragraph about that person, using logical organization.

Writing Trait

Organize your **paragraph** by putting ideas in an order that makes sense.

Student Model

Writer uses quotation marks to indicate words from story.

Details support idea that Elena is determined.

> Elena knows what she wants, and she works to reach her goals. She tells Papa she wants to be a glassblower. He tells her that girls cannot do that job. Elena is "mad as a wet hen," but she doesn't give up. She dresses like a boy and walks across the desert to a factory. Some people might be scared of desert animals, but Elena helps them all. When the factory men laugh at her, Elena blows glass and surprises them. Finally, Elena works with Papa, making her dream come true.

Paragraph has organization: topic sentence, followed by details and a conclusion.

Use the model to help you write your own good paragraph.

402

Hints for Writing Good Paragraphs

- Write an opening sentence that "sets up" your topic or main idea and engages readers. Consider a topic sentence, a question, or an interesting fact.
- Use transition words and phrases such as *first, after, but, also, however, then, for example,* and *on the other hand* to connect ideas, sentences, and paragraphs.
- Make sure each sentence in the paragraph supports the topic or main idea.
- Write a conclusion that wraps things up but is more than a repeating of ideas or "The end."

Social Studies
in Reading

Expository Nonfiction

Genre
- **Expository nonfiction explains specific details of a topic.**
- **Expository nonfiction gives facts in a clear, organized way.**

Text Features
- **Maps or other graphics are often used to show where events took place.**

Link to Social Studies

Use the library or the Internet to research other people who worked on or used the Underground Railroad to escape slavery. Share what you learn in a brief report.

LEADING PEOPLE TO FREEDOM

BY JULIA NASSER PADGETT

It is one thing to follow your own dream of freedom. It is quite another to bravely risk that freedom to help others be free. Harriet Tubman did just that. Harriet Tubman was born into slavery in Maryland in 1820. Slavery is the owning of a person by another person. When she was a child, Harriet Tubman was sent away from her family to work in the fields. There she heard other slaves talk about wanting to be free. It was then that Harriet Tubman first heard of the Underground Railroad. It wasn't a real railroad with trains and stations, however. The Underground Railroad was a secret system that provided slaves with help and the opportunity to escape slavery and find freedom.

To keep things as secret as possible, the Underground Railroad even had its own code language. The "trains" were the people who were running to freedom. The "conductors" were the people who led slaves on their journey to parts of the northern United States and Canada. The "stations" were churches, homes, and stores of free African Americans and white people who believed that slavery was wrong.

Predict Can you make a prediction about Harriet Tubman?

When she was 29 years old, Harriet Tubman used the Underground Railroad to escape from slavery. She did this by walking through the cold woods at night and by getting help from people at the stations. She finally found freedom when she arrived in Philadelphia. When she discovered what it meant to be free, she wanted to lead other slaves to freedom. She soon began working on the Underground Railroad.

Harriet Tubman risked her life on 19 trips to help over 300 slaves find freedom, including her family. She showed courage by facing danger without fear. She used this courage and her intelligence to outwit the slave owners. Harriet Tubman spent her life helping African Americans build new lives in freedom.

UNDERGROUND RAILROAD ROUTES

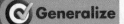 **Generalize** Make a generalization about the Underground Railroad.

Reading Across Texts

Harriet Tubman and Elena each showed courage in seeking a certain freedom. What freedom did each want?

Writing Across Texts Write a brief paragraph explaining each freedom, and tell which means the most to you.

The Star-Spangled Banner

by Francis Scott Key

Oh say, can you see, by the dawn's
    early light,
What so proudly we hailed at the twilight's
    last gleaming—
Whose broad stripes and bright stars,
    through the perilous fight,
O'er the ramparts we watched were so
    gallantly streaming!
And the rocket's red glare, the bombs
    bursting in air,
Gave proof through the night that our flag
    was still there;
Oh! say, does that star-spangled banner
    yet wave
O'er the land of the free, and the home
    of the brave!

I Watched an Eagle Soar

by **Virginia Driving Hawk Sneve**

Grandmother,
I watched an eagle soar
high in the sky
until a cloud covered him up.
Grandmother,
I still saw the eagle
behind my eyes.

Words Free as Confetti

by Pat Mora

Come, words, come in your every color.
I'll toss you in storm or breeze.
I'll say, say, say you,
taste you sweet as plump plums,
bitter as old lemons.
I'll sniff you, words, warm
as almonds or tart as apple-red,
feel you green
and soft as new grass,
lightwhite as dandelion plumes,
or thorngray as cactus,
heavy as black cement,
cold as blue icicles,
warm as *abuelita's* yellowlap.
I'll hear you, words, loud as searoar's
purple crash, hushed
as *gatitos* curled in sleep,
as the last goldlullaby.

I'll see you long and dark as tunnels,
bright as rainbows,
playful as chestnutwind.
I'll watch you, words,
rise and dance and spin.
I'll say, say, say you
in English,
in Spanish,
I'll find you.
Hold you.
Toss you.
I'm free too.
I say *yo soy libre,*
I am free
free, free,
free as confetti.

411

Wrap-Up

What Freedom Means to Me

People often use bumper stickers to make a short statement about something that is important to them. Plan a bumper sticker with your own personal statement of what it means to be free. Write it on a strip of paper in neat writing. Add a small picture if you like.

What does it mean to be free?

Lessons on Freedom

connect to
WRITING

As you learned from the selections in this unit, freedom means different things to different people. Complete a chart like the one below to show what each character learned about freedom. Then choose one character whose view of freedom is most like yours. Write about what you learned about freedom from this selection or character.

Character	What freedom means to him/her	Experience that caused this

Make a Mural Plan

connect to
ART

In *Talking Walls: Art for the People,* you read about many artists who use murals to express ideas or themes that are important to them. Work with a group to plan a mural about freedom. First, talk over ideas you have for the mural. Next, make a sketch. Then talk about any changes you want to make. Finally, transfer your sketch to a large piece of paper and color it in.

Genre Study

What do you like to read? Fables? Poetry? Expository nonfiction? Select a favorite genre and do a study. For example, a genre study of fantasy might compare *Wings* with *Elena's Serenade*.

Try It

- Define the genre.
- Set up a chart with special features of the genre.
- Read two or more examples of the genre.
- Compare selections and complete the chart.

A fantasy is a made-up story that could never happen.

Selection	Characters	Setting	Fantastic Elements
Wings by Christopher Myers	Ikarus Jackson I (narrator)	city	A boy who has wings can fly.
Elena's Serenade by Campbell Geeslin	Elena Papa glassblowers	Mexico	When Elena plays music, magical things happen.

A chart for historical fiction might have headings such as these: Title, Topic, Historical Facts, and Fictional Elements.

Author Study

Do you have a favorite selection? Make a note of the author's name and look for books by that author. You will probably enjoy other works by him or her.

Try It

- Find three or four works by one author.
- Read the book jackets or use the Internet to learn about the author's life to see what may have influenced his or her writing.
- Read the author's works.
- Compare topics, genres, and so on.
- Tell which work is your favorite and why.

Read this author study of Steve Jenkins.

Steve Jenkins

Steve Jenkins has always liked science and art. As a child he kept spiders and lizards. He also liked to draw and paint. In his books, Mr. Jenkins tries to make science fun. "Kids have a natural interest in animals and things like volcanoes," he said. My favorite book by Steve Jenkins is <u>Hottest, Coldest, Highest, Deepest</u> because it answers questions that I want to know about.

Meet Authors of Expository Nonfiction and Photo Essay

Katacha Díaz
The author of *Talking Walls*, p. 336

Katacha Díaz grew up in Peru and immigrated to the United States when she was 15. She was one of seven daughters. Her parents moved to the United States so that the girls could get a good education. Moving to a new country as a teenager was hard. "My sister Ana María and I were the only Spanish-speaking students in our new school. There was a lot of peer pressure to get rid of the accent," she says. Murals have always fascinated Ms. Díaz. She especially loves the murals by Paul and David Botello because they speak of education, immigration, and hope. These themes are a big part of her own life. "Education is important in my family," she points out. **Other books about murals: *The School Mural* and *Murals: Walls That Sing***

Steve Jenkins
The author of *Hottest, Coldest, Highest, Deepest*, p. 40

Steve Jenkins has always liked science and art. As a child he kept spiders and lizards. He also liked to draw and paint. His father was a scientist. "We did a lot of projects together," he said. "We wrote a little book about animals." In his books, Mr. Jenkins tries to make science fun. "Kids have a natural interest in animals and things like volcanoes," he said. He wrote *Hottest, Coldest, Highest, Deepest* partly because his son was always asking him those kinds of questions. The pictures in Mr. Jenkins's books are not drawings or paintings. They are called collages. Collages are made by cutting different kinds of paper and pasting them in layers. **Other books: *The Top of the World* and *What Do You Do with a Tail Like This?***

Meet Authors of Biography

David Adler
The author of *America's Champion Swimmer*, p. 90

David Adler has written almost two hundred books! He was the first person to write a book about Gertrude Ederle. "I read every newspaper and magazine story I could find about her," he says. Some newspapers said a woman could never swim the English Channel. Mr. Adler has five brothers and sisters. "My parents encouraged each of us to be an individual. As a child I was known as the family artist." Paintings and drawings he did then still hang in his parents' home. "I've always been a dreamer," Mr. Adler says. He recently spoke with his fourth-grade teacher. She remembered the time she went to the principal. "What should I do with Adler?" she asked. "He's always dreaming." "Leave him alone," the principal said. "Maybe one day he'll become a writer." **Other books: *The Babe and I* and *A Picture Book of Harriet Beecher Stowe***

Carol Otis Hurst
The author of *Rocks in His Head*, p. 64

As a child, Carol Otis Hurst went to the library almost every day. Later, Ms. Hurst became a school librarian herself. She even taught classes about children's books. People sometimes asked her why she hadn't written a book. "I had a lot of family stories in my head. A couple of those stories began to take shape." *Rocks in His Head* was Ms. Hurst's first book. It is the true story of her father. "He collected rocks from the time he was a small boy. He kept at it throughout his life, not caring that others thought it was a waste of time." Ms. Hurst says her father loved to learn new things. "He'd be thrilled to think kids at school were reading about him." **Other books about unique people: *Snowflake Bentley* and *Beethoven Lives Upstairs***

Meet Authors of Realistic Fiction

Claire Hartfield

The author of *Me and Uncle Romie*, p. 248

Claire Hartfield began taking dance lessons when she was five. Dance is her way to tell stories. In *Me and Uncle Romie*, she wanted to show how an artist can use art to tell stories. Although *Me and Uncle Romie* is fiction, it is based on the life of collage artist Romare Bearden. Today, Ms. Hartfield is a lawyer in Chicago. **Other books about art: *Loo-Loo, Boo and Art You Can Do* and *Recycled Crafts Box***

Frances Park and Ginger Park

The authors of *Good-Bye, 382 Shin Dang Dong*, p. 198

Frances and Ginger Park are sisters. They often work as a team to create a book. Together, they have written books for both children and adults. Although their parents came from Korea, Frances and Ginger Park were born near Washington, D.C. The sisters own a chocolate shop. People often stop by to talk about their books. "We pack up their truffles, and then talk books," says Frances. **Other books: *Where on Earth Is My Bagel?* and *My Freedom Trip***

Susan L. Roth

The author/illustrator of *Happy Birthday Mr. Kang*, p. 308

Susan L. Roth got the idea for *Happy Birthday Mr. Kang* from a newspaper story. She read about a group of Chinese men who brought their *hua mei* birds to the park each Sunday. Ms. Roth went to the park to check it out. "It was very noisy," she said. "They were clearly communicating with each other." **Other books: *The Biggest Frog in Australia* and *How Thunder and Lightning Came to Be***

Meet Authors of Realistic Fiction

Chieri Uegaki
The author of *Suki's Kimono*, p. 150

Chieri Uegaki began writing at the age of seven when she published a family newspaper called *The Pender Street Times*. At the time, she lived on Pender Street in Vancouver, British Columbia. Ms. Uegaki says about her writing: "It makes me very happy to think that something I've written could touch someone and perhaps even become someone's favorite." Ms. Uegaki based *Suki's Kimono* on her relationship with her Japanese grandmother. Ms. Uegaki offers this advice to young writers: "Listen more than you speak. Read everything and take notes." **Other books about children like Suki:** *First Day, Hooray!* **and** *It's Back to School We Go!*

Natasha Wing
The author of *Jalapeño Bagels*, p. 224

Natasha Wing lives in northern California, where she often buys jalapeño bagels at a bakery in town. The bakery, called Los Bagels Bakery and Café, gave Ms. Wing the idea for this story. Los Bagels offers many tasty snacks, such as Mexican hot chocolate, pumpkin turnovers, and bagels topped with jalapeño jelly. Ms. Wing is married and has two cats, Toonces and Jemima, and a dog named Sabaka. **Another book:** *The Night Before Summer Vacation*

Meet Authors of Narrative Nonfiction

Susan Kuklin

The author/photographer of *How My Family Lives in America*, p. 174

Susan Kuklin combines photos and words in her books. *How My Family Lives in America* is from a series of books she did to show what children are thinking and feeling. Ms. Kuklin wanted to show how families give children a sense of identity. She says, "Sanu, Eric, and April took great pride in teaching me about who they are and what makes their families distinctive. It has been a joy to know them." The words in the book were spoken by the children. Ms. Kuklin wrote them down and shaped them into a book.
Other books: *Dance* and *From Head to Toe: How a Doll Is Made*

Betsy and Giulio Maestro

The author and illustrator of *The Story of the Statue of Liberty*, p. 288

Betsy and Giulio Maestro are husband and wife. They have published more than one hundred books together! Ms. Maestro says, "We work on so many interesting books about so many different topics that we're always learning new things." Ms. Maestro feels a special connection to the Statue of Liberty. Her grandmother saw the statue for the first time as she arrived at Ellis Island from Russia in 1918. Because Ms. Maestro grew up in New York City, she visited the Statue of Liberty many times. On a class field trip, she even climbed to the crown. **Other books: *The New Americans* and *The Story of Money***

Meet Authors of Fantasy and Animal Fantasy

Campbell Geeslin
The author of *Elena's Serenade*, p. 384

Campbell Geeslin grew up in western Texas. He writes the first draft of his stories in longhand on a yellow pad of paper. After he edits his work, he puts it into a word processor. One of Mr. Geeslin's stories, *How Nanita Learned to Make Flan*, has been made into an opera. Mr. Geeslin wrote the libretto (the words that are sung) for the opera. **Other books: *In Rosa's Mexico* and *On Ramón's Farm***

Christopher Myers
The author/illustrator of *Wings*, p. 16

Christopher Myers is an award-winning author and illustrator of children's books. He uses cut paper, photographs, wallpaper, woodcuts, and paint to illustrate his stories. Mr. Myers's father, Walter Dean Myers, is a famous children's author. At first Christopher helped his father by doing research for him. Then he illustrated one of his father's books. Later they worked as a team on another book. Now Mr. Myers writes and illustrates his own books. **Other books: *Fly* and *Black Cat***

Chris Van Allsburg
The author/illustrator of *Two Bad Ants*, p. 358

Chris Van Allsburg says that in grade school other kids thought it was cool that he could draw. But in junior high, he stopped drawing. Learning how to play football seemed more important. Thankfully, Mr. Van Allsburg changed his mind. In college he took some art classes. That decision changed his life. He loved his art so much that he sometimes forgot his other classes. **Other books: *The Wreck of the Zephyr* and *Just a Dream***

Antonio L. Castro

The illustrator of *Jalapeño Bagels*, p. 224

Antonio L. Castro has illustrated many children's books. He is also an artist. His art has been displayed in museums in Texas, Mexico, Spain, and Italy. Mr. Castro was born in Zacatecas, Mexico. He now lives in Juarez, Mexico, and is considered one of the best artists in the El Paso-Juarez area. He teaches art and local history classes to children in museums and libraries near his home. **Another book: *Pájaro Verde/The Green Bird***

Niki Daly

The illustrator of *Fly, Eagle, Fly!* p. 116

Niki Daly was born in Cape Town, South Africa, and he lives there today. His picture books have won awards all over the world. Mr. Daly uses watercolors with pen or pencil to create his lively pictures. For his books, Mr. Daly says he first watches people. Then he draws his characters many times, "until they become as real as the people around me." As a child, Mr. Daly read a lot of comic books. They taught him to tell stories through pictures. In his books, Mr. Daly tries to show children of all races. Mr. Daly also likes to write songs. He has even recorded two albums.

Other books: *Old Bob's Brown Bear* and *Jamela's Dress*

Ana Juan
The illustrator of *Elena's Serenade*, p. 384

Ana Juan lives in Spain. She has done many kinds of art, but she loves drawing illustrations for children's books. She says, "Working on a picture book gives you more possibilities to explain in better and more detail the different moments and events around a life." **Other books about following dreams: *Girl Wonder* and *Muffler Man***

Jerome Lagarrigue
The illustrator of *Me and Uncle Romie*, p. 248

Jerome Lagarrigue grew up in Paris, France, in a family of artists. His art has appeared in magazines, and he has illustrated several picture books. Mr. Lagarrigue teaches drawing and painting in New York City. For *Me and Uncle Romie*, he used some elements of collage in his paintings—like Romare Bearden.

James Stevenson
The illustrator of *Rocks in His Head*, p. 64

James Stevenson has written and illustrated more than one hundred children's books. More than thirty of them have won awards. Mr. Stevenson knew he wanted to be a writer. But his first success was with cartoons. He wrote his first children's book with his eight-year-old son. "Tell me a story, and we'll make a book," he told his son, James. "He stood at my desk and told a story. I wrote it down and then did the pictures." They called the book *If I Owned a Candy Factory*. It was published in 1968. **Other books: *Corn Chowder* and *It's Raining Pigs and Noodles***

Glossary

How to Use This Glossary

This glossary can help you understand and pronounce some of the words in this book. The entries in this glossary are in alphabetical order. There are guide words at the top of each page to show you the first and last words on the page. A pronunciation key is at the bottom of every other page. Remember, if you can't find the word you are looking for, ask for help or check a dictionary.

The entry word is in dark type. It shows how the word is spelled and how the word is divided into syllables.

The pronunciation is in parentheses. It also shows which syllables are stressed.

Part-of-speech labels show the function or functions of an entry word and any listed form of that word.

a·dore (ə dôr′), VERB. to love and admire someone very greatly: *She adores her mother.* ❑ VERB. **a·dores, a·dored, a·dor·ing.**

Sometimes, irregular and other special forms will be shown to help you use the word correctly.

The definition and example sentence show you what the word means and how it is used.

Aa

ad·mire (ad mīr′), VERB. to look at with wonder, pleasure, and approval: *We all admired the beautiful painting.* ❑ VERB **ad·mires, ad·mired, ad·mir·ing.**

air·port (âr′pôrt′), NOUN. an area used regularly by aircraft to land and take off. An airport has buildings for passengers and for keeping and repairing aircraft.

at·tempt (ə tempt′), VERB. to try: *She attempted to climb the mountain.* ❑ VERB **at·tempts, at·tempt·ed, at·tempt·ing.**

at·ten·tion (ə ten′shən), NOUN. careful thinking, looking, or listening: *Give me your attention while I explain this math problem.*

at·tic (at′ik), NOUN. the space in a house just below the roof and above the other rooms.

av·er·age (av′ər ij), NOUN. the quantity found by dividing the sum of all the quantities by the number of quantities. The average of 3 and 5 and 10 is 6 (because $3 + 5 + 10 = 18$, and 18 divided by $3 = 6$).

Bb

bak·er·y (bā′kər ē), *NOUN.* a place where bread, pies, cakes, and pastries are made or sold.

batch (bach), *NOUN.* a quantity of something made at the same time: *a batch of cookies.*

board (bôrd), **1.** *NOUN.* a broad, thin piece of wood for use in building: *We used 10-inch boards for shelves.* **2.** *NOUN.* a group of people managing something; council: *a board of directors.*

boil (boil), *VERB.* to cause a liquid to bubble and give off steam by heating it: *He boils some water for tea.* ❑ *VERB* **boils, boiled, boil·ing.**

bow (bou), *VERB.* to bend the head or body in greeting, respect, worship, or obedience: *The people bowed before the queen.* ❑ *VERB* **bows, bowed, bow·ing.**

braid·ed (brād′ed), *ADJECTIVE.* woven or twined together: *The warm, braided bread was delicious.*

bur·ro (bėr′ō), *NOUN.* a donkey used to carry loads or packs in the southwestern United States and Mexico.

burros

burst (bėrst), *VERB.* to break open or be opened suddenly: *The trees had burst into bloom.* ❑ *VERB* **bursts, burst·ed, burst·ing.**

a in hat	ō in open	sh in she
ā in age	ȯ in all	th in thin
â in care	ô in order	ŦH in then
ä in far	oi in oil	zh in measure
e in let	ou in out	ə = a in about
ē in equal	u in cup	ə = e in taken
ėr in term	u̇ in put	ə = i in pencil
i in it	ü in rule	ə = o in lemon
ī in ice	ch in child	ə = u in circus
o in hot	ng in long	

Cc

can·vas (kan′vəs), *NOUN.* a strong, heavy cloth made of cotton. It is used to make tents, sails, and certain articles of clothing, and for artists' paintings.

card·board (kärd′bôrd′), *NOUN.* a stiff material made of layers of paper pulp pressed together, used to make cards, posters, boxes, and so on.

cel·e·brate (sel′ə brāt), *VERB.* to do something special in honor of a special person or day: *We celebrated my birthday with a party.* ❑ *VERB* **cel·e·brates, cel·e·brat·ed, cel·e·brat·ing.**

celebrate

chill·y (chil′ē), *ADJECTIVE.* cold; unpleasantly cool: *It is a rainy, chilly day.*

chore (chôr), *NOUN.* a small task or easy job that you have to do regularly: *Feeding our pets is one of my daily chores.* ❑ *PLURAL* **chores.**

clam·ber (klam′bər), *VERB.* to climb something, using your hands and feet; scramble: *We clambered up the cliff.* ❑ *VERB* **clam·bers, clam·bered, clam·ber·ing.**

clog (klog), *NOUN.* a shoe with a thick, wooden sole.

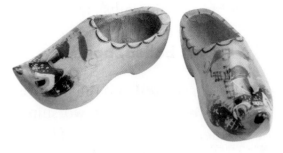

clogs

clutch (kluch), *VERB.* to grasp something tightly: *I clutched the railing to keep from falling.* ❑ *VERB* **clutch·es, clutched, clutch·ing.**

426

col·lage (kə läzh′), NOUN. a picture made by pasting things such as parts of photographs, newspapers, fabric, and string onto a background.

collage

com·plain (kəm plān′), VERB. to say that you are unhappy, annoyed, or upset about something: *We complained that the room was too cold.* ❑ VERB **com·plains, com·plained, com·plain·ing.**

con·tin·ue (kən tin′yü), **1.** VERB. to keep up; keep on; go on: *The rain continued all day.* **2.** VERB. to go on with something after stopping for a while: *The story will be continued next week.* ❑ VERB **con·tin·ues, con·tin·ued, con·tin·u·ing.**

cot·ton (kot′n), ADJECTIVE. cloth made from soft, white fibers that grow in fluffy bunches on the cotton plant: *I like to wear cotton in hot weather.*

cou·ra·geous (kə rā′jəs), ADJECTIVE. full of courage; fearless; brave.

crev·ice (krev′is), NOUN. a narrow split or crack: *Tiny ferns grew in crevices in the stone wall.* ❑ PLURAL **crev·ic·es.**

crown (kroun), NOUN. a head covering of precious metal worn by a royal person, such as a queen or a king.

crys·tal (kris′tl), NOUN. a hard, solid piece of some substance that is naturally formed of flat surfaces and angles. Crystals can be small, like grains of salt, or large, like some kinds of stone.

a in hat	ō in open	sh in she
ā in age	ȯ in all	th in thin
â in care	ô in order	ᴛʜ in then
ä in far	oi in oil	zh in measure
e in let	ou in out	ə = a in about
ē in equal	u in cup	ə = e in taken
ėr in term	ù in put	ə = i in pencil
i in it	ü in rule	ə = o in lemon
ī in ice	ch in child	ə = u in circus
o in hot	ng in long	

cur·i·ous (kyùr′ē əs), *ADJECTIVE.* strange; odd; unusual: *I found a curious, old box in the attic.*

cur·rent (kėr′ənt), **1.** *NOUN.* a flow or stream of water, electricity, air, or any fluid: *The current swept the stick down the river.* **2.** *ADJECTIVE.* of or about the present time: *current events.*

cus·tom (kus′təm), *NOUN.* an old or popular way of doing things: *The social customs of many countries differ from ours.*

cus·tom·er (kus′tə mər), *NOUN.* someone who buys goods or services: *Just before the holidays, the store was full of customers.*

Dd

de·li·cious (di lish′əs), *ADJECTIVE.* very pleasing or satisfying; delightful, especially to the taste or smell: *a delicious cake.*

depth (depth), *NOUN.* the distance from the top to the bottom: *The depth of the well is about 25 feet.*

de·scribe (di skrīb′), *VERB.* to tell in words how someone looks, feels, or acts, or to record the most important things about a place, a thing, or an event: *The reporter described the awards ceremony in detail.* ❑ *VERB* **de·scribes, de·scribed, de·scrib·ing.**

des·ert (dez′ərt), *NOUN.* a dry, sandy region without water and trees: *In northern Africa there is a great desert called the Sahara.*

desert

de·ter·mined (di tėr′mənd), *ADJECTIVE.* with your mind made up: *Her determined look showed that she had decided what to do.*

dis·ap·pear (dis′ə pir′), *VERB.*
to vanish completely; stop
existing: *When spring came, the snow
disappeared.* ❑ *VERB* **dis·ap·pears,
dis·ap·peared, dis·ap·pear·ing.**

dis·cov·er·y (dis kuv′ər ē), *NOUN.*
something found out: *One of Benjamin
Franklin's discoveries was that lightning
is electricity.*

dough (dō), *NOUN.* a soft, thick
mixture of flour, liquid, and other
things from which bread, biscuits,
cake, and pie crusts are made.

drift (drift), *VERB.* to carry or be
carried along by currents of air or
water: *A raft drifts if it is not steered.*
❑ *VERB* **drifts, drift·ed, drift·ing.**

drown (droun), *VERB.* to die or cause
to die under water or other liquid
because of lack of air to breathe: *We
almost drowned when our boat overturned.*
❑ *VERB* **drowns, drowned,
drown·ing.**

Ee

ech·o (ek′ō), *VERB.* to be heard again:
Her shout echoed through the valley. ❑ *VERB*
ech·oes, ech·oed, ech·o·ing.

en·cour·age (en kėr′ij), *VERB.* to give
someone courage or confidence;
urge on: *We encouraged our team with
loud cheers.* ❑ *VERB* **en·cour·ag·es,
en·cour·aged, en·cour·ag·ing.**

encourage

a	in hat	ō	in open	sh	in she
ā	in age	ȯ	in all	th	in thin
â	in care	ô	in order	ᵺ	in then
ä	in far	oi	in oil	zh	in measure
e	in let	ou	in out	ə	= a in about
ē	in equal	u	in cup	ə	= e in taken
ėr	in term	u̇	in put	ə	= i in pencil
i	in it	ü	in rule	ə	= o in lemon
ī	in ice	ch	in child	ə	= u in circus
o	in hot	ng	in long		

en·thu·si·as·tic (en thü′zē as′tik), *ADJECTIVE.* eagerly interested; full of enthusiasm: *My little brother is enthusiastic about going to kindergarten.*

ex·pres·sion (ek spresh′ən), *NOUN.* the act of putting into words or visual medium: *freedom of expression.*

Ff

fab·ric (fab′rik), *NOUN.* a woven or knitted material; cloth. Velvet, denim, and linen are fabrics. ❏ PLURAL **fab·rics.**

fac·to·ry (fak′tər ē), *NOUN.* a building or group of buildings where people and machines make things.

fa·mous (fā′məs), *ADJECTIVE.* very well known; noted: *The famous singer was greeted by a large crowd.*

fare·well (fâr′wel′), *ADJECTIVE.* parting; last: *a farewell kiss.*

feast (fēst), *NOUN.* a big meal for a special occasion shared by a number of people: *The breakfast that she cooked was a real feast.*

fes·ti·val (fes′tə vəl), *NOUN.* a program of entertainment, often held annually: *a summer music festival.*

festival

fierce (firs), *ADJECTIVE.* wild and frightening: *The fierce lion paced in his cage.*

fierce

flight¹ (flīt), *NOUN.* a set of stairs from one landing or one story of a building to the next. ❏ PLURAL **flights.**

flight² (flīt), *NOUN.* act of fleeing; running away; escape; *The flight of the prisoners was discovered.*

fool·ish (fü′lish), *ADJECTIVE.* without any sense; unwise: *It is foolish to cross the street without looking both ways.*

fo·reign (fôr′ən), *ADJECTIVE.* outside your own country: *She travels often in foreign countries.*

fra·grant (frā′grənt), *ADJECTIVE.* having a sweet smell or odor: *These cinnamon buns are very fragrant.*

Gg

gawk (gȯk), *VERB.* to stare at someone or something in a rude way; gape: *People driving by gawked at the accident.* ❑ *VERB* **gawks, gawked, gawk·ing.**

gig·gle (gig′əl), *NOUN.* a silly or uncontrolled laugh.

gin·ger·ly (jin′jər lē), *ADVERB.* with extreme care or caution: *He walked gingerly across the ice.*

glar·ing (glâr′ing), *ADJECTIVE.* staring angrily.

glass·blow·er (glas blō′ər), *NOUN.* a person who shapes glass objects by blowing air from the mouth through a tube into a blob of hot, liquid glass at the other end of the tube.

glassblowers

glum (glum), *ADJECTIVE.* gloomy; dismal; sad: *I felt very glum when my friend moved away.*

a in hat	ō in open	sh in she
ā in age	ȯ in all	th in thin
â in care	ô in order	ᴛʜ in then
ä in far	oi in oil	zh in measure
e in let	ou in out	ə = a in about
ē in equal	u in cup	ə = e in taken
ėr in term	u̇ in put	ə = i in pencil
i in it	ü in rule	ə = o in lemon
ī in ice	ch in child	ə = u in circus
o in hot	ng in long	

goal (gōl), *NOUN.* something desired: *Her goal was to be a scientist.*

grace·ful (grās′fəl), *ADJECTIVE.* beautiful in form or movement: *He is a graceful dancer.*

gul·ly (gul′ē), *NOUN.* a ditch made by heavy rains or running water.

Hh

hand·ker·chief (hang′kər chif), *NOUN.* a soft, usually square piece of cloth used for wiping your nose, face, or hands.

her·it·age (her′ə tij), *NOUN.* traditions, skills, and so on, that are handed down from one generation to the next; inheritance: *Freedom is our most precious heritage.*

home·sick (hōm′sik′), *ADJECTIVE.* very sad because you are far away from home.

hov·er (huv′ər), *VERB.* to stay in or near one place in the air: *The two birds hovered over their nest.* ❑ *VERB* **hov·ers, hov·ered, hov·er·ing.**

Ii

ig·nore (ig nôr′), *VERB.* to pay no attention to something or someone: *The driver ignored the traffic light and almost hit another car.* ❑ *VERB* **ig·nores, ig·nored, ig·nor·ing.**

in·gre·di·ent (in grē′dē ənt), *NOUN.* one of the parts of a mixture: *The ingredients of a cake usually include eggs, sugar, flour, and flavoring.* ❑ *PLURAL* **in·gre·di·ents.**

ingredient

in·ter·na·tion·al (in′tər nash′ə nəl), *ADJECTIVE.* between or among two or more countries: *A treaty is an international agreement.*

Jj

jan•i•tor (jan′ə tər), *NOUN*. someone whose work is taking care of a building or offices. Janitors do cleaning and make some repairs.

jour•ney (jėr′nē), *NOUN*. a long trip from one place to another: *I'd like to take a journey around the world.*

joy•ful (joi′fəl), *ADJECTIVE*. causing or showing joy; glad; happy: *joyful news.*

Kk

knead (nēd), *VERB*. to press or mix together dough or clay into a soft mass: *The baker was kneading dough to make bread.* ❑ *VERB* **kneads, knead•ed, knead•ing.**

knead

Ll

la•bel (lā′bəl), *VERB*. to put or write a label on something: *She labeled her backpack with her name and address.* ❑ *VERB* **labels, labeled, label•ing.**

lib•er•ty (lib′ər tē), *NOUN*. freedom: *In 1865, the United States granted liberty to all people who were enslaved.*

lo•cal (lō′kəl), *ADJECTIVE*. about a certain place, especially nearby, not far away: *I go to a local doctor.*

loop (lüp), *VERB*. to form a line, path, or motion shaped so that it crosses itself: *The plane looped twice in the air above the ground.* ❑ *VERB* **loops, looped, loop•ing.**

a in hat	ō in open	sh in she
ā in age	ȯ in all	th in thin
â in care	ô in order	ᴛʜ in then
ä in far	oi in oil	zh in measure
e in let	ou in out	ə = a in about
ē in equal	u in cup	ə = e in taken
ėr in term	u̇ in put	ə = i in pencil
i in it	ü in rule	ə = o in lemon
ī in ice	ch in child	ə = u in circus
o in hot	ng in long	

433

Mm

med·al (med′l), *NOUN*. a piece of metal like a coin, given as a prize or award. A medal usually has a picture or words stamped on it: *She received two medals in gymnastics.* ❑ *PLURAL* **med·als.**

mem·or·y (mem′ər ē), *NOUN*. a person, thing, or event that you can remember: *One of my favorite memories is my seventh birthday party.* ❑ *PLURAL* **mem·or·ies.**

men·tion (men′shən), *VERB*. to tell or speak about something: *I mentioned your idea to the group that is planning the picnic.* ❑ *VERB* **men·tions, men·tioned, men·tion·ing.**

min·er·al (min′ər əl), *NOUN*. a solid substance, usually dug from the Earth. Minerals often form crystals. Coal, gold, sand, and mica are minerals. Some minerals, such as iron, sodium, and zinc, are nutrients. ❑ *PLURAL* **min·er·als.**

mix·ture (miks′chər), *NOUN*. a mixed condition: *At the end of the move, I felt a mixture of relief and disappointment.*

mod·el (mod′l), *NOUN*. a small copy of something: *A globe is a model of the Earth.* ❑ *PLURAL* **mod·els.**

mur·al (myŭr′əl), *NOUN*. a large picture painted on a wall. ❑ *PLURAL* **mur·als.**

mural

Nn

narrow (nar′ ō), *ADJECTIVE*. not wide; having little width; less wide than usual for its kind: *a narrow path.*

narrow

na·tive (nā′tiv), *ADJECTIVE*. belonging to someone because of that person's birth: *The United States is my native land.*

Oo

out·run (out run′), *VERB*. to run faster than someone or something: *She can outrun her older sister.* ❑ *VERB* **out·runs, out·ran, out·run·ning.**

o·ver·night (ō′vər nīt′), *ADVERB*. during the night: *She likes to stay overnight with friends.*

Pp

pace (pās), *NOUN*. a step: *He took three paces into the room.* ❑ *PLURAL* **pac·es.**

pale (pāl), *ADJECTIVE*. not bright; dim: *a pale blue.*

peak (pēk), *NOUN*. the pointed top of a mountain or hill: *We saw the snowy peaks in the distance.*

ped·es·tal (ped′i stəl), *NOUN*. a base on which a column or a statue stands.

pedestal

perch (pėrch), *VERB*. to come to rest on something; settle; sit: *A robin perches on the branch.* ❑ *VERB* **perch·es, perched, perch·ing.**

a in hat	ō in open	sh in she
ā in age	ȯ in all	th in thin
â in care	ô in order	ᴛʜ in then
ä in far	oi in oil	zh in measure
e in let	ou in out	ə = a in about
ē in equal	u in cup	ə = e in taken
ėr in term	ù in put	ə = i in pencil
i in it	ü in rule	ə = o in lemon
ī in ice	ch in child	ə = u in circus
o in hot	ng in long	

pitch·er[1] (pich′ər), *NOUN.* a container made of china, glass, or silver, with a lip at one side and a handle at the other. Pitchers are used for holding and pouring out water, milk, and other liquids.

pitch·er[2] (pich′ər), *NOUN.* a player on a baseball team who pitches to the catcher. The batter tries to hit the ball before it gets to the catcher.

pitcher

pla·teau (pla tō′), *NOUN.* a large, flat area in the mountains or high above sea level.

pop·u·lar (pop′yə lər), *ADJECTIVE.* liked by most people: *a popular song.*

pos·ses·sion (pə zesh′ən), *NOUN.* something owned; property: *Please move your possessions from my room.*
❑ *PLURAL* **pos·ses·sions.**

pre·cip·i·ta·tion (pri sip′ə tā′shən), *NOUN.* the amount of water that falls from the air in a certain time.

pub·lic (pub′lik), *ADJECTIVE.* of or for everyone; belonging to the people: *public libraries.*

puff (puf), *VERB.* to swell up: *He puffs up his cheeks when he plays his trumpet.*
❑ *VERB* **puffs, puffed, puff·ing.**

pum·per·nick·el (pum′pər nik′əl), *NOUN.* a kind of rye bread. It is dark and firm.

Qq

quar·ry (kwôr′ē), *NOUN.* a place where stone is dug, cut, or blasted out for use in putting up buildings.
❑ *PLURAL* **quar·ries.**

Rr

rain·drop (rān′drop′), *NOUN.* the water that falls in drops from the clouds. ❑ *PLURAL* **rain·drops.**

rec·i·pe (res′ə pē), *NOUN.* a set of written directions that show you how to fix something to eat: *Please give me your recipe for bread.*

reed (rēd), *NOUN.* a kind of tall grass that grows in wet places. Reeds have hollow, jointed stalks. ❑ *PLURAL* **reeds.**

reeds

re·luc·tant·ly (ri luk′tənt lē), *ADVERB.* unwillingly.

re·ply (ri plī′), *VERB.* to answer someone by words or action: *He replied with a shout.* ❑ *VERB* **re·plies, re·plied, re·ply·ing.**

res·i·dent (rez′ə dənt), *NOUN.* someone living in a place, not just a visitor: *The residents of the town are proud of its new library.* ❑ *PLURAL* **res·i·dents.**

rhythm (riᴛʜ′əm), *NOUN.* the natural strong beat that some music or poetry has. Rhythm makes you want to clap your hands to keep time.

riv·et (riv′it), *VERB.* to fasten something with metal bolts. ❑ *VERB* **riv·ets, riv·et·ed, riv·et·ing.**

ru·in (rü′ən), *VERB.* to destroy or spoil something completely: *The rain ruined our picnic.* ❑ *VERB* **ru·ins, ru·ined, ru·in·ing.**

a	in hat	ō	in open	sh	in she
ā	in age	ȯ	in all	th	in thin
â	in care	ô	in order	ᴛʜ	in then
ä	in far	oi	in oil	zh	in measure
e	in let	ou	in out	ə	= a in about
ē	in equal	u	in cup	ə	= e in taken
ėr	in term	ů	in put	ə	= i in pencil
i	in it	ü	in rule	ə	= o in lemon
ī	in ice	ch	in child	ə	= u in circus
o	in hot	ng	in long		

437

Ss

scoop (sküp), *NOUN.* a tool like a small shovel used to dip up things. A cuplike scoop is used to dish up ice cream.

scram·ble (skram′bəl), *VERB.* to make your way, especially by climbing or crawling quickly: *We scrambled up the steep, rocky hill, trying to follow the guide.* ❑ *VERB* **scram·bles, scram·bled, scram·bling.**

sculp·tor (skulp′tər), *NOUN.* an artist who makes things by cutting or shaping them. Sculptors make statues of marble, bronze, and so on.

sculptor

se·re·nade (ser′ə nād′), *NOUN.* music played or sung; tune.

set·tle (set′l), *VERB.* to set up the first towns and farms in an area: *The English settled New England.* ❑ *VERB* **set·tles, set·tled, set·tling.**

shriek (shrēk), *VERB.* to make a loud, sharp, shrill sound. People sometimes shriek because of terror, anger, pain, or joy. ❑ *VERB* **shrieks, shrieked, shriek·ing.**

sleek (slēk), *ADJECTIVE.* soft and shiny; smooth: *sleek hair.*

snick·er (snik′ər), *VERB.* to laugh in a sly, silly way: *The children snickered to each other.* ❑ *VERB* **snick·ers, snick·ered, snick·er·ing.**

snug (snug), *ADJECTIVE.* fitting your body closely: *That coat is a little too snug.*

so·cial (sō′shəl), *ADJECTIVE.* concerned with human beings as a group: *Schools and hospitals are social institutions.*

sou·ve·nir (sü′və nir′), *NOUN.* something given or kept as a reminder; keepsake: *She bought a pair of moccasins as a souvenir of her trip out West.*

spare (spâr), **1.** *ADJECTIVE.* extra: *a spare tire.* **2.** *VERB.* to show mercy to someone; decide not to harm or destroy: *He spared his enemy's life.* ❏ *VERB* **spares, spared, spar·ing.**

stamp (stamp), **1.** *NOUN.* a small piece of paper with glue on the back; postage stamp. You put stamps on letters or packages before mailing them. ❏ *PLURAL* **stamps. 2.** *VERB.* to bring down your foot with force: *He stamped his foot in anger.* ❏ *VERB* **stamps, stamped, stamp·ing.**

stir (stèr), **1.** *VERB.* to mix something by moving it around with a spoon, stick, and so on: *Stir the sugar into the lemonade.* **2.** *VERB.* to move something: *The wind stirred the leaves.* ❏ *VERB* **stirs, stirred, stir·ring.**

stoop¹ (stüp), *NOUN.* a forward bend of the head and shoulders: *My uncle walks with a stoop.*

stoop² (stüp), *NOUN.* a porch or platform at the entrance of a house. ❏ *PLURAL* **stoops.**

stroke (strōk), **1.** *NOUN.* the act of hitting something; blow: *I drove in the nail with several strokes of the hammer.* **2.** *NOUN.* a single complete movement made over and over again: *He rowed with strong strokes of the oars.*

strug·gle (strug′əl), *VERB.* to try hard; work hard against difficulties: *The swimmer struggled successfully against the tide.* ❏ *VERB* **strug·gles, strug·gled, strug·gling.**

sum·mit (sum′it), *NOUN.* the highest point; top: *We climbed to the summit of the mountain.*

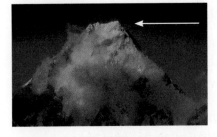

summit

a in hat	ō in open	sh in she
ā in age	ò in all	th in thin
â in care	ô in order	ᴛʜ in then
ä in far	oi in oil	zh in measure
e in let	ou in out	ə = a in about
ē in equal	u in cup	ə = e in taken
ėr in term	ù in put	ə = i in pencil
i in it	ü in rule	ə = o in lemon
ī in ice	ch in child	ə = u in circus
o in hot	ng in long	

439

sup·port (sə pôrt′), *VERB.* to help; aid: *Parents support and love their children.* ❑ *VERB* **sup·ports, sup·port·ed, sup·port·ing.**

swoop (swüp), *VERB.* to come down fast on something, as a hawk does when it attacks: *Bats are swooping down from the roof of the cave.* ❑ *VERB* **swoops, swooped, swoop·ing.**

sym·bol (sim′bəl), *NOUN.* an object, diagram, icon, and so on, that stands for or represents something else: *The olive branch is the symbol of peace.*

Tt

tab·let (tab′lit), *NOUN.* a small, flat surface with something written on it.

tempt (tempt), *VERB.* to appeal strongly to; attract: *That cake is tempting me.* ❑ *VERB* **tempts, tempt·ed, tempt·ing.**

tide (tīd), *NOUN.* the rise and fall of the ocean about every twelve hours. This rise and fall is caused by the gravitational pull of the moon and the sun. ❑ *PLURAL* **tides.**

torch (tôrch), *NOUN.* a long stick with material that burns at one end of it.

torch

tra·di·tion (trə dish′ən), *NOUN.* a custom or belief handed down from parents to children. ❑ *PLURAL* **tra·di·tions.**

treas·ure (trezh′ər), *NOUN.* any person or thing that is loved or valued a great deal: *The silver teapot is my parents' special treasure.*

tune (tün), *NOUN.* a piece of music; melody: *popular tunes.*

twi·light (twī′līt′), *NOUN.* the faint, soft light reflected from the sky after sunset.

twist (twist), *NOUN.* a braid formed by weaving together three or more strands of hair, ribbon, or yarn: *She wore her hair in a twist at the back of her head.*

Uu

un·a·ware (un′ə wâr′), *ADJECTIVE*. not aware; unconscious: *We were unaware of the approaching storm.*

un·for·get·ta·ble (un′fər get′ə bəl), *ADJECTIVE*. so good or so wonderful that you cannot forget it: *Winning the race was an unforgettable experience.*

un·veil (un vāl′), *VERB*. to remove a veil from; uncover; disclose; reveal: *She unveiled her face.* ❑ *VERB* **un·veils, un·veiled, un·veil·ing.**

Vv

val·ley (val′ē), *NOUN*. a region of low land that lies between hills or mountains. Most valleys have rivers running through them.

valley

vi·o·lent·ly (vī′ə lənt lē), *ADVERB*. acting or done with great force: *He violently signaled for the train to stop.*

Ww

wa·ter·fall (wȯ′tər fȯl′), *NOUN*. a stream of water that falls from a high place. ❑ *PLURAL* **wa·ter·falls.**

waterfall

a	in hat	ō	in open	sh	in she
ā	in age	ȯ	in all	th	in thin
â	in care	ô	in order	ᴛʜ	in then
ä	in far	oi	in oil	zh	in measure
e	in let	ou	in out	ə	= a in about
ē	in equal	u	in cup	ə	= e in taken
ėr	in term	u̇	in put	ə	= i in pencil
i	in it	ü	in rule	ə	= o in lemon
ī	in ice	ch	in child	ə	= u in circus
o	in hot	ng	in long		

Unit 4

Wings

English	Spanish
attention	atención
complained	quejarse
drifting	flotando
giggle	risita
glaring	mirada feroz
looping	dando la vuelta
struggled	tuvo dificultad
swooping	volando en picado

Hottest, Coldest, Highest, Deepest

English	Spanish
average	promedio
depth	profundidad
deserts	desiertos
outrun	correr más rápido que
peak	cima
tides	mareas
waterfalls	cataratas

Rocks in His Head

English	Spanish
attic	ático
board	consejo
chores	quehaceres
customer	cliente
labeled	rotuló
spare	de repuesto
stamps	estampillas

America's Champion Swimmer: Gertrude Ederle

English	Spanish
celebrate	celebrarán
continued	siguió
current	corriente
drowned	se ahogó
medals	medallas
stirred	revolvió
strokes	brazadas

Fly, Eagle, Fly!

English	Spanish
clutched	agarraron
echoed	hicieron eco
gully	barranco
reeds	juncos
scrambled	luchó por salir
valley	valle

Unit 5

Suki's Kimono

English	Spanish
cotton	algodón
festival	festival
graceful	elegante
handkerchief	pañuelo
paces	pasos
pale	claro
rhythm	ritmo
snug	ceñido

How My Family Lives in America

English	Spanish
admire	admirar
custom	costumbre
famous	famoso
mention	mencione
overnight	durante la noche
popular	popular
public	pública
twist	moño

Good-Bye, 382 Shin Dang Dong

English	Spanish
airport	aeropuerto
curious	curiosa
delicious	deliciosa
described	descrito
farewell	despedida
homesick	nostálgico
memories	memorias
raindrops	gotas de lluvia

Jalapeño Bagels

English	Spanish
bakery	panadería
batch	hornada
boils	hierva
braided	trenzado
dough	masa
ingredients	ingredientes
knead	amasa
mixture	mezcla

Me and Uncle Romie

English	Spanish
cardboard	cartón
feast	festín
fierce	feroz
flights	tramos (de escalera)
pitcher	lanzador
ruined	arruinado
stoops	pórticos
treasure	tesoro

444

Unit 6

The Story of the Statue of Liberty

English	Spanish
crown	corona
liberty	libertad
models	maquetas
symbol	símbolo
tablet	lápida
torch	antorcha
unforgettable	inolvidable
unveiled	descubrió

Talking Walls: Art for the People

English	Spanish
encourages	anima
expression	expresión
local	locales
native	natales
settled	se asentaron
social	sociales
support	apoyar

Happy Birthday Mr. Kang

English	Spanish
bows	inclina
chilly	frío
foolish	tonto
foreign	extranjero
narrow	estrechas
perches	se posa
recipe	receta

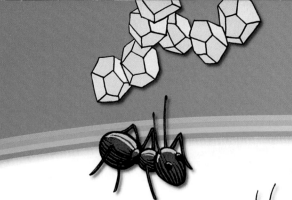

Two Bad Ants

English	Spanish
crystal	cristal
disappeared	desapareció
discovery	descubrimiento
goal	meta
journey	viaje
joyful	alegres
scoop	cucharilla
unaware	no se dieron cuenta

Elena's Serenade

English	Spanish
burro	burro
bursts	explota
factory	fábrica
glassblower	soplador de vidrio
puffs	infla
reply	respondo
tune	melodía

446

Acknowledgments

Text

16: updated From *Wings* by Christopher Myers. Published by Scholastic Press/Scholastic Inc. Copyright © 2000 by Christopher Myers. Reprinted by permission; **40:** From *Hottest, Coldest, Highest, Deepest* by Steve Jenkins. Copyright © 1998 by Steve Jenkins. Reprinted by permission of Houghton Mifflin Company. All rights reserved; **56:** Excerpt from *Factastic Book of Comparisons* by Russell Ash. Text copyright © 1997 Russell Ash. Compilation and illustrations © 1997 Dorling Kindersley Limited, London. Reprinted by permission; **64:** *Rocks in His Head* by Carol Otis Hurst. Text copyright © 2001 by Carol Otis Hurst. Used by permission of HarperCollins Publishers; **78:** From *Everybody Needs a Rock.* Text copyright © 1974 by Byrd Baylor. Reprinted with permission of Atheneum Books for Young Readers, Simon & Schuster Children's Publishing Division. All rights reserved; **90:** Text from *America's Champion Swimmer: Gertrude Ederle,* copyright © 2000 by David A. Adler, reprinted by permission of Harcourt, Inc. Illustrations from *America's Champion Swimmer: Gertrude Ederle* by David A. Adler, illustrations, copyright © 2000 by Terry Widener, reproduced by permission of Harcourt, Inc.; **108:** "Women Athletes" from Women in History: Wilma Rudolph website, www.lkwdpl.org. Courtesy of Women In History, www.lkwdpl.org/wihohio; **116:** From *Fly, Eagle, Fly!* Text copyright © 2000 by Christopher Gregorowski. Illustrations copyright © 2000 by Niki Daly. Reprinted with permission of Margaret K. McElderry Books, an Imprint of Simon & Schuster Children's Publishing Division. All rights reserved; **132:** (Updated) *Purple Coyote* by Cornette, Illustrated by Rochette. Copyright © 1997 by L'Ecole des Loisirs, Paris. First American edition 1999–Originally published in France by Pastel, 1997. English translation copyright © 1999 by Random House Inc. Published by arrangement with Random House Children's Books, a division of Random House, Inc. New York, New York. All rights reserved. Reprinted by permission; **138:** From *Because I Could Not Stop My Bike* by Karen Jo Shapiro. Text copyright © 2003 by Karen Jo Shapiro. Illustration copyright © 2003 by Matt Faulkner. Used with permission of Charlesbridge Publishing, Inc. All rights reserved; **139:** (Updated) "By Myself" from *Honey, I Love* by Eloise Greenfield. Text Copyright © 1978 by Eloise Greenfield. Used by permission of HarperCollins Publishers. Reprinted by permission of Nancy Gallt Literary Agency; **141:** "Written at the Po-Shan Monastery" by Hsin Ch'i-chi, translated by Irving Y. Lo from Sunflower Splender edited by Liu, Wu-chi and Irving Yucheng Lo, 1990. Reprinted by permission of Indiana University Press; **150:** *Suki's Kimono* written by Chieri Uegaki and Illustration by Stéphane Jorisch, is used with the permission of Kids Can Press, Ltd., Toronto. www.kidscanpress.com. Text © 2003 Chieri Uegaki. Illustrated © 2003 Stéphane Jorisch; **174:** From *How My Family Lives in America.* Copyright © 1992 by Susan Kuklin. Reprinted with permission of Simon & Schuster Books for Young Readers, Simon & Schuster Children's Publishing Division. All rights reserved; **192:** From *Scott Foresman Social Studies Communities 2003.* Copyright © 2003 Pearson Education, Inc. Reprinted by permission of Pearson Education, Inc.; **198:** (Updated) Reprinted with permission of the National Geographic Society from *Good-Bye, 382 Shin Dang Dong* by Frances Park and Ginger Park. Copyright © 2002 Frances Park and Ginger Park. Illustrations © 2002 Yangsook Choi; **218:** (Updated) Lyrics from *It's a Small World* by Richard M. Sherman & Robert B. Sherman. Words and Music by Richard M. Sherman and Robert B. Sherman. © 1963 Wonderland Music Company, Inc. Reproduced by permission; **224:** From *Jalapeño Bagels.* Copyright © 1996 by Natasha Wing. Reprinted with permission of Atheneum Books for Young Readers, Simon & Schuster Children's Publishing Division. All rights reserved; **240:** "A Happy Heart", "Native Foods", and "The Spanish Flavor" from *Viva Mexico! - The Foods* by George Ancona, 2002. Reprinted with permission of Marshall Cavendish; **248:** From *Me and Uncle Romie: A Story Inspired by the Life and Art of Romare Bearden* by Claire Hartfield, illustrated by Jerome Lagarrigue, copyright © 2002 by Claire Hartfield, text. Used by permission of Dial Books for Young Readers, A Division of Penguin Young Readers Group, A Member of Penguin Group (USA) Inc., 345 Hudson Street, New York, NY 10014. All rights reserved; **272:** (Updated) www.FactMonster.com. © Pearson Education, published as FactMonster.com; **276:** "My Friend in School" from *DeShawn Days.* Text copyright © 2001 by Tony Medina. Permission arranged with Lee & Low Books Inc., New York NY 10016; **278:** "Lunch Survey", from *Swimming Upstream: Middle Grade Poems* by Kristine O'Connell George. Text copyright © 2002 by Kristine O'Connell George. Reprinted by permission of Clarion Books, an imprint of Houghton Mifflin Company. All rights reserved; **279:** "Saying Yes" is copyright by Diana Chang. Reprinted by permission of the author; **288:** *The Story of the Statue of Liberty* by Betsy C. Maestro, illustrations by Maestro Giulio. Text copyright © 1986 by Betsy Maestro. Illustrations copyright © 1986 by Giulio Maestro. Used by permission of HarperCollins Publishers; **302:** From *Scott Foresman Social Studies Communities 2003.* Copyright © 2003 Pearson Education, Inc. Reprinted by permission of Pearson Education, Inc.; **308:** From *Happy Birthday Mr. Kang* by Susan L. Roth. Copyright © 2001 Susan L. Roth. Reprinted with permission of the National Geographic Society; **352:** (Updated) "Nathaniel's Rap" from *Nathaniel Talking* by Eloise Greenfield. Copyright © 1988 by Eloise Greenfield. Reprinted by permission of Gallt Literary Agency; **358:** (Updated) *Two Bad Ants* by Chris Van Allsburg. Copyright © 1988 by Chris Van Allsburg. Reprinted by permission of Houghton Mifflin Company. All rights reserved; **384:** From *Elena's Serenade.* Text copyright © 2004 by Campbell Geeslin. Illustrations copyright © 2004 by Ana Juan. Reprinted with permission of Atheneum Books for Young Readers, Simon & Schuster Children's Publishing Division. All rights reserved; **409:** "I Watched an Eagle Soar" from *Dancing Teepees: Poems of the North American Indian Youth* by Virginia Driving Hawk Sneve. Copyright © 1989 by Virginia Driving Hawk Sneve. Reprinted from *Dancing Teepees: Poems* by permissions of Holiday House, Inc.; **410:** "Words Free as Confetti" from *Confetti: Poems for Children.* Text copyright © 1996 by Pat Mora. Permission arranged with Lee and Low Books, Inc., New York, NY 10016.

Illustrations

Cover: ©Mark Buehner; **4, 10, 142-143** Bill Mayer; **13-15** Kris Wiltse; **30-35** Kyle Still; **78-85, 194-195** Franklin Hammond; **113, 355** Scott Gustafson; **145, 224-238, 439** Antonio Castro; **147-149** Shelly Hehenberger; **171** Chris Lensch; **218** Sachiko Yoshikawa; **276-278** Laurie Keller; **352-353** Jan Spivey Gilchrist; **404-406** Neil Shigley; **408-410** Stephen Daigle; **435** Teresa Flavin; **436** Wendell Minor.

Photography

Every effort has been made to secure permission and provide appropriate credit for photographic material. The publisher deeply regrets any omission and pledges to correct errors called to its attention in subsequent editions.

Unless otherwise acknowledged, all photographs are the property of Scott Foresman, a division of Pearson Education.

Photo locators denoted as follows: Top (T), Center (C), Bottom (B), Left (L), Right (R), Background (Bkgd).

6 (TR) ©Jeremy Horner/Getty Images, (TC) ©Royalty-Free/ Corbis; **8** ©1991/Faith Ringgold; **16** Getty Images; **28** Getty Images; **37** (TR) ©Comstock, Inc., (BR) ©Royalty-Free/Corbis; **38** ©Dale Wilson/Masterfile Corporation; **39** (T) Getty Images, (TC) ©Ken Welsh/Age Fotostock, (BR) ©Royalty-Free/Corbis; **56** (TC, TR, CC) Getty Images, (BR) ©James Balog/Getty Images; **59** (BR, TR) Getty Images; **61** (TR) Brand X Pictures, (BR) ©Jonathan Blair/Corbis, (TR) ©Richard T. Nowitz/ Corbis; **62** ©Maurice Nimmo/Frank Lane Picture Agency/ Corbis; **63** (TL) ©Bill Ross/Corbis, (TR) ©Art Wolfe/Getty Images, (BR) ©Richard T. Nowitz/Corbis; **80** ©Art Wolfe/ Getty Images; **87** ©Creasource/ Masterfile Corporation; **88** Brand X Pictures; **89** (T) ©Bill Bachmann/PhotoEdit, (BC) ©David Young-Wolff/PhotoEdit; **108** (TR) ©Underwood & Underwood/Corbis, (BC) ©George Silk/Time Life Pictures/ Getty Images; **110** ©George Silk/Time Life Pictures/Getty Images; **111** (CL) ©George Silk/Time Life Pictures/Getty Images, (CR) ©Bettmann/Corbis; **114** Getty Images; **115** (TR, BR) ©Royalty-Free/Corbis; **144** ©Jeremy Horner/Getty Images; **166** (BR) Getty Images, (BC) ©Christie's Images/ Peter Harholdt/Corbis, (BR) Art Resource, NY; **167** (TR) Art Resource, NY, (CR) ©Lynn Goldsmith/Corbis; **168** (TR) ©Historical Picture Archive/Corbis, (CR) ©Werner Forman/ Corbis, (BR) Getty Images; **169** (CR) Getty Images, (TR) Corbis, (BR) ©Pavlovsky Jacques/Corbis; **172** Getty Images; **173** Getty Images; **174** Getty Images; **179** Jupiter Images; **182** Getty Images; **185** (BR) ©Creative Concept/Index Stock Imagery; **190** (TL, BR) Getty Images; **192** (BR) Morton Beebe/ Corbis, (TR) Getty Images; **193** (BR) ©Steve Vidler/SuperStock, (TR) Getty Images; **196** ©Ed Bock/Corbis; **197** (TR) ©Tom Stewart/Corbis, (TC) Getty Images; **221** (T, BL) Getty Images, (CR) ©Royalty-Free/ Corbis; **222** Getty Images; **223** ©Royalty-Free/Corbis; **240-243** George Ancona; **245** (TL) ©Alan Schein Photography/ Corbis, (TR, CR) Getty Images; **246** Getty Images; **247** Getty Images; **272** (TR) ©Terry W. Eggers/Corbis, (BR) ©David Zimmerman/Corbis; **273** AP/Wide World Photos; **274** ©Duomo/Corbis; **275** (CR) ©David Thomas/PictureArts/ Corbis, (BR) ©Royalty-Free/Corbis; **280** ©Jeremy Horner/ Getty Images; **282** ©1991/Faith Ringgold; **283** (CR) "Reach High and You Will Go Far" © 2000 Art and Photography by Joshua Sarantitis. All Rights Reserved. Sponsored by the Philadelphia Mural Arts Program; **285** (TL) Corbis, (TR) ©Royalty-Free/Corbis, (BR) Getty Images; **286** ©Richard Berenholtz/Corbis; **287** ©Gail Mooney/Corbis; **302** (TR) ©Bettmann/Corbis, (CC) ©Jim Erickson/Corbis Stock Market; **303** ©Robert Holmes/Corbis; **306** ©Royalty-Free/ Corbis; **307** Getty Images; **328** (TC) ©Steve Kaufman/Corbis, (R) ©Darrell Gulin/Corbis; **329** (TL) ©Erik Freeland/Corbis, (BR) ©Claus Meyer/Minden Pictures; **330** (TL) ©Jeff Vanuga/ Corbis, (BL) ©Comstock Inc.; **331** (T) ©Jim Zipp/Photo Researchers, Inc., (BR) ©Jeff Vanuga/Corbis; **333** (T) ©Matthias Kulka/Corbis, (T) Getty Images; **337** ©Meg Saligman; **339** ©Ben Valenzuela; **340-341** ©Hector Ponce/Rich Puchalsky; **343** (C) "Reach High and You Will Go Far" ©2000 Art and Photography by Joshua Sarantitis. All Rights Reserved. Sponsored by the Philadelphia Mural Arts Program; **344** ©Paul Botello; **346** Getty Images; **347** ©David Botello; **348** Courtesy of the U.S. Capitol Historical Society; **349** (TL, B) ©Meg Saligman; **357** (T) ©M. Bahr/Peter Arnold, Inc., (CC) ©Michael & Patricia Fogden/Corbis; **378** ©Ron Watts/Corbis; **379** ©Royalty-Free/Corbis; **381** (T) ©K. M. Westermann/ Corbis, (TC) ©James L. Amos/Corbis; **382** ©Kelly-Mooney Photography/Corbis; **383** ©George B. Diebold/Corbis; **412** ©1991/Faith Ringgold; **413** ©1991/Faith Ringgold; **419** Courtesy, Kids Can Press; **421** (C) ©Scholastic, Inc., (T) Philip Groshong/©Cincinatti Opera; **422** Photo of Niki Daly used with permission of Simon & Schuster, Inc.; **423** ©Ana Juan; **431** ©Walt Anderson/Visuals Unlimited; **432** (BL) ©Lawrence Migdale, (BR) Getty Images; **434** The National Park Service; **436** ©Robert Lindholm/Visuals Unlimited; **437** ©K. M. Westermann/Corbis; **438** ©Jeff Greenberg/Visuals Unlimited; **439** ©Vincent Besnault/Stone/Getty Images; **440** SuperStock; **441** Getty Images; **442** ©AFP/Getty Images; **443** ©Bob Stefko/ Imagebank/Getty Images; **444** ©Manfred Rutz/Taxi/Getty Images; **445** ©Galen Rowell/Corbis; **446** ©David Madison/ Imagebank/Getty Images; **447** SuperStock; **448** Getty Images.

Glossary

The contents of the glossary have been adapted from *Thorndike Barnhart School Dictionary*, copyright © 2001, Pearson Education, Inc.